ENDORSEMENTS

Soul Shapers represents a startling discovery that has implications for Adventist teachers and school administrators. If effectively describes the elements of William Glasser's choice theory, draws comparisons to the writings of Ellen White, and presents practical examples of how student behavior situations are effectively facilitated by both of these writers' concepts. *Soul Shapers* is a valuable treatise on achieving desirable student behavior, particularly as it relates to the removal of coercion and control. It emphasizes that the most important thing in student behavior is not the result, but the process.

—Gerald N. Kovalski
Vice President for Education
North American Division of Seventh-day Adventists

∞

Soul Shapers will help Adventist educators refocus their efforts in reaching God's kids as it reaffirms our Adventist philosophy of education. Drawing on firsthand experiences as a teacher, principal, and superintendent, the author shares practical stories that model the preferred practices that all parents and teachers can utilize to improve the awesome task of developing our youth into spiritual champions. This book connects the dots, clearly showing the alignment between Ellen White's principles of Christian education and William Glasser's concepts of quality schools.

—Dennis Plubell
Associate Director of Education
North Pacific Union Conference of Seventh-day Adventists
Chair, North American Division of Seventh-day Adventists
"Journey to Excellence" Development Committee

Soul Shapers releases the power of Ellen White in this fresh manuscript that boldly places her words beside a highly respected modern educational philosopher. The new insights drawn from this comparison will revolutionize the way we do education in Adventist schools.

—Sandra Doran, Ed.D.
Associate Superintendent of Education
Florida Conference of of Seventh-day Adventists

The work of Ellen G. White, our inspired founder, more than 100 years ago established guidelines and a philosophy for our education work. William Glasser, considering modern education from a significantly different perspective, has arrived at many similar concepts and practices that are revolutionizing classrooms and learning environments around the world. Together these two authors provide a clear focus for changing the grade-oriented, seat-time, coercive school environment into a success-oriented, competency-based, inviting environment that could lead to dramatic improvements in student outcomes. *Soul Shapers* compares and contrasts their theories and practices and could lead us to significant improvements in our education program. Our challenge is to transform our schools into Adventist Christian quality schools.

—Kelly Bock Ed.D.
Director of Education
Pacific Union Conference of Seventh-day Adventists

When the principles presented in this book are thoroughly understood and employed in our schools and homes, we can expect to see a dramatic difference in our young people. They will learn to become self-controlled as they are taught without the use of coercion or manipulation. *Soul Shapers* presents this material in an interesting and friendly way.

—Beth Bursey
Curriculum Specialist
Florida Conference of Seventh-day Adventists

Interesting and well-written, *Soul Shapers* will help parents, teachers, and other caring adults to develop meaningful, noncoercive relationships with the young people in their lives, and in the process help them to become responsible, caring, and successful adults.

—Sharon Searson
Associate Superintendent of Education
Upper Columbia Conference of Seventh-day Adventists

A book whose ideas could revolutionize our thinking and our doing in the areas of teaching, parenting, and leading. *Soul Shapers* demonstrates how our understanding of choice and freedom, God's unique gifts to human beings, can lead to "quality" schools and homes. A must-read for anyone (not just teachers and parents) who is searching for a model and approach to achieve internal motivation!

—Elissa Kido, Ed.D.
Dean, School of Education
La Sierra University

Soul Shapers is essential for every Seventh-day Adventist educator who wants students to become thinkers and not reflectors of others' thoughts, morally responsible human beings, and persons with the power to change the world. As I read this book, I grew increasingly excited with its potential to change forever the direction of Adventist education toward lasting and positive results. Following this "better plan" would do more than anything else to leave the back door of the church virtually unused.

—Jean Sheldon, Ph.D.
Associate Professor of Religion
Pacific Union College
Angwin, California
Pacific Union Conference of Seventh-day Adventists

JIM ROY

Soul Shapers

A Better Plan for Parents and Educators

REVIEW AND HERALD® PUBLISHING ASSOCIATION
HAGERSTOWN, MD 21740

Texts credited to NIV are from the *Holy Bible, New International Version.* Copyright ©
1973, 1978, 1984, International Bible Society. Used by permission of Zondervan Bible
Publishers.

Texts credited to NKJV are from the New King James Version. Copyright © 1979,
1980, 982 by Thomas Nelson, Inc. Used by permission. All rights reserved.

Scripture quotations marked NLT are from the *Holy Bible,* New Living Translation,
copyright © 1996. Used by permission of Tyndale House Publishers, Inc., Wheaton,
Illinois 60184. All rights reserved.

Bible texts credited to RSV are from the Revised Standard Version of the Bible, copyright © 1946, 1952, 1971, by the Division of Christian Education of the National Council
of the Churches of Christ in the U.S.A. Used by permission.

This book was
Edited by Raymond H. Woolsey
Copyedited by Delma Miller
Cover design by Ron J. Pride/square1studio
Cover photo by Photos.com
Interior design by Candy Harvey
Electronic makeup by Shirley M. Bolivar
Typeset 11/13 Bembo

PRINTED IN U.S.A.

09 08 07 06 05   5 4 3 2 1

R&H Cataloging Service
Roy, Jim, 1954–   .

Soul shapers: a better plan for parents and educators.

1. Moral education.   2. Education—Aims and objectives. 3. Christian
education.   4. Glasser, William.

I. Title.

370.114

ISBN 0-8280-1831-6

To order additional copies of *Soul Shapers*, by Jim Roy, **call 1-800-765-6955.**
Visit us at **www.reviewandherald.com** for information on other
Review and Herald® products.

DEDICATION

To
Ed Boyatt and
Dick and Anita Molstead,
thank you.

And to the many educators they represent,
who continually strive for
the success of their students.

ACKNOWLEDGMENTS

This book is a better read because of the help of my wife, Maggie. As my best friend, she was interested in what I was writing; and as my "editor," she gave good advice that helped the ideas to flow better and to make better sense.

The support of our children, Rachel and Jordan, meant more to me than they probably know. Their interest in the project and their consistent encouragement was a source of inspiration.

I owe much to my good friend and fellow educator, Tom Amato. He, too, read chapters of the manuscript and gave very specific and helpful feedback. More than that, though, he has been a soul mate for many years and has helped to shape and refine my thinking. Many of the ideas in this book have been modeled to me by Tom.

Along the way there have been a number of people who became aware of "the better plan" project and supported me in a variety of ways. The following is not a complete list, but it includes people such as Sharon Searson, Dave Escobar, Kelly Bock, Beth Bursey, Elissa Kido, Martha Havens, Jeff Tirengel, Linda Harshman, Anita Oliver, Fred Kinsey. Heidi Decena, Sarah Harris, Rich Ehlers, Vern Jeske, Barbara Thompson, and Sarah Lausevic.

A special acknowledgment must go to the people I have worked with over the years. We worked through challenges together—some of them extremely difficult—and for their support I will always be indebted. We also celebrated successes together and experienced the joy that results when ideas and plans actually work. Besides former colleagues, I am also thinking of the many wonderful school parents who were willing to listen to new ideas and throw their support into new directions.

Finally, I want to thank Jeannette Johnson at the Review and Herald Publishing Association for seeing the importance of these ideas, and for walking a first-time author through the many details that led to this book being in your hand right now.

Contents

FOREWORD

Several years ago I made a major talk to the educational branch of the Seventh-day Adventist Church. Before my presentation, I met Jim Roy at the hotel. We made a connection, and I have been close to him ever since. I presented my choice theory ideas to these educators and explained how they could not only be the theory behind all of my psychological and educational work but also the core of how I lead my personal life.

As I got to know Jim, he made me aware of how much he believed that my ideas follow very closely the nearly 100-year-old educational teachings of Ellen White. I had heard from others that she had taught many of the same concepts, but it was not until I got close to Jim that I realized how much our educational thinking coincided, even though our family backgrounds were very different.

What is so amazing is that I don't believe I would have to change any of the ways I think and teach to keep this coincidence intact. I am pleased that the choice theory I teach has become part of the training for a group of Seventh-day Adventist schools that are working to become Glasser Quality Schools. I am pleased that, inadvertently, I may have made more Adventist teachers aware of Ellen White's important work because of what Jim Roy has pointed out so eloquently in this book.

—William Glasser

INTRODUCTION

This book is about a vitally important process: the process of helping our children and our students become adults who are <u>spiritually connected,</u> <u>emotionally strong</u>, and <u>socially skilled</u>. The process, if we are to believe Ellen White and William Glasser, is full of paradoxes. It seems we must do the opposite of what our common sense tells us to do.

Calling on White and Glasser to guide us through these paradoxes may seem like a strange pair to team up, but the comparison of their ideas seems clear to me—even striking. It is true that Glasser writes from a secular humanist perspective and, thus, believes in the ability of the human race to improve itself and succeed on its own, while Ellen White writes from a sacred perspective and believes the human race must be rescued by a loving Savior. Their theoretical foundations are extremely different, yet several of their key points are very much the same. Of course, you will need to decide for yourself the extent to which you agree with these similarities. This book simply invites you to consider what they are saying.

Recently I gave a presentation that compared the ideas of White and Glasser to a mixed group made up of educators and psychologists and counselors. There were Seventh-day Adventists in the group, but most were not. At the end of my talk, I opened it up for questions, and the first one came from a prominent psychologist who asked me, "Why do you need Glasser?" This took me by surprise since I was, if anything, expecting questions such as "Who is Ellen White?" (I later learned that the psychologist who asked the question is a close friend of Glasser and strongly supports his ideas.) The question hung in the air: *Why do you need Glasser?* Really, the question was a compliment to the clarity of Ellen White's writing. Glasser himself one time shared with me that "<u>if the Adventists listened to what Ellen White says, they'd be fine</u>."

And so this book attempts to inform us about the key ideas, beliefs, and themes that Glasser and White urge us to consider. Chapters 1 and 2 give a background on how the idea for this book got started, and explain that there are specific elements that do, indeed, lead to success at school and at home. Chapters 3, 4, 5, and 6 describe the beliefs that parents, teachers, and principals will embrace that prepare the way for this success. In other words, what we think leads to how we behave, so these first chapters (3-6) focus on beliefs and thinking. Chapters 7, 8, and 9 focus on behavior. If a school or home believes as White and Glasser describe, what would their strategies and actions look like? Chapter 10 challenges us to believe as Mrs. White and other educational theorists describe, and to develop school approaches that match those beliefs.

I am convinced that accepting this challenge will result in more effective and more joyful schools and homes. It is probably true that few of us have experienced a non-coercive environment, but I believe the principles described in this book appeal to something that God has planted deep within us. Over the years, as I have talked with educators and parents, they have expressed great interest in this approach. I would very much like to hear your response to these ideas, or to answer any questions you have. I owe much of my present understanding to the influence that others have had on me, and I recognize that my understanding has not arrived, but that it continues to develop.

To that end, I can be reached at: thebetterplan@sbcglobal.net.

 # Discovery

"The rung of a ladder was never meant to rest upon, but only to hold a man's foot long enough to enable him to put the other somewhat higher."—Thomas Huxley.

The multipurpose room was filled with more people than we had expected, although, to be honest, we weren't sure how many to expect. The evening program had been titled "Cooperative Learning for Parents" and was meant to be a workshop for parents interested in finding out about a learning format that their students were experiencing at school. A number of the staff had worked together to plan the evening. We wanted those attending to not just hear a description of cooperative learning, but to actually experience it, to feel what it was like to work through a challenge with other team members. Although highly effective when implemented correctly, cooperative learning formats are easily misunderstood. We wanted to answer questions and help parents understand and ultimately support our teaching efforts.

The evening went well. Except for a certain small pocket of attendees, parents enjoyed the group activities and asked questions to help them understand the learning strategy better. They were truly having a good time, partly because the activities were fun as well as challenging, and partly because they were getting to see fellow parents that they had not seen for a while. There is something almost magical about cooperative learning and what it can bring out in people. People who are used to sitting passively and listening to the teacher lecture from up front can become quite involved with the learning and with each other when given a chance to do so.

The "small pocket" was a bit of a different story, though, and in their defense I offer this explanation. The state legislature of this particular state had voted to make sweeping changes in public school standards, and many people were fearful of what these changes would mean to their children. In effect, the changes created an outcome-based curriculum that was intended to "raise the learning bar" and emphasize accountability. Many felt that what the legislature was doing was indeed necessary and good, but others felt that the legislature was making decisions they had no business making.

The feelings ran deep enough that when it came to these school decisions there was a charged atmosphere whenever educational topics were brought up. Many felt that the changes were intrusive, controlling, and arbitrary. A large number of religious parents felt that the state was getting involved in areas that should be left to parents to decide.

So when we came together on this evening to present our reasons for being enthusiastic, confident, and supportive of cooperative learning, most were happy at what they were experiencing, but a few came with the baggage of the state educational turmoil. They entered the multipurpose room that night with doubts and suspicions, eager to make sure that we did not try to pull something over their eyes and harm their children in the process. As the evening progressed, it was easy to pick up on their frustration and even anger. Others seemed to ignore the feelings of this group, but several of us couldn't help noticing their tension. Little did I realize that one of them would have a profound effect on me, and that it would come in a form that I never would have expected.

We were almost to the end of the scheduled time for the workshop and I was up front summarizing the school's goals, sharing our motives, and answering questions. I had been learning about and implementing cooperative learning for more than six years and had attended workshops and classes, read and studied a lot of cooperative learning resource books and materials, and had met and visited with a number of the leaders in the cooperative learning field, including David and Roger Johnson and Spencer Kagan. One of the authors I had become familiar with in my reading was William Glasser, who had written a book entitled *The Quality School* (1990).

I had read the book a couple years before and had even shared his ideas with several staff members. They had responded positively. Glasser believes that one of the components of a quality school is to teach strategies that use student learning teams. That is, students will often learn together as assignments and projects are completed as a team effort. As part of my summarizing comments I referred to William Glasser and a few of the principles he wrote about in *The Quality School*. His ideas were a part of our motivation, and I wanted parents to understand where we were coming from as a school and where we wanted to go.

As I was sharing I noticed a hand raised and saw that it was a member of the "small pocket." She had a look of frustration on her face, combined with determination. When I called on her, in a tone laced with frustration she said, "I don't know why we have to go to secular authors when we have the red books."[1] I acknowledged her concern and tried to point out the reasons that we were interested in the Quality School approach. As a school staff we looked at ourselves as strong supporters of the Spirit of Prophecy,[2] and any changes in the school program that we considered would need to pass through the "red books" filter. I tried to say that in my response to her, but I don't think I was very articulate or clear.

The workshop concluded shortly after that, and many parents came up to me and the other teachers and thanked us for a wonderful, informative evening. They encouraged us to use cooperative learning strategies in our classrooms and expressed appreciation for our wanting to provide the best learning experiences possible for their children. A few told us not to worry about the "small pocket" and to just keep heading the direction we were heading.

But as good as the evening had gone, and even with the affirmation that we received from appreciative parents, it was that one statement from the frustrated parent that stuck with me. I found myself thinking defensively, reviewing my commitment to the writings of Ellen White, reviewing decisions that we had made that reflected that commitment, or considering the writing of William Glasser and how what he espoused was a good thing for students, teachers, and schools. In effect, she had passed her frustration to me, because now I wanted the ability to be clear and articulate on a topic that I felt was very important.

Almost six months later I was in my office, studying before a staff worship that I was scheduled to give that morning. It was early, and the school still had a special quiet, the kind of quiet that exists before the teachers arrived one by one, before the copy machine started churning out classroom assignments and newsletters, before the phone started ringing with requests of every kind, and before the buses pulled up in front and unloaded 175 diverse students, bringing life once again to the slumbering buildings. I was actually reading through sections of one of the "red books," *Fundamentals of Christian Education,* when my eyes fell on a passage that caused me to pause, look at it again, and reread it carefully. I paused again, only to re-peat that cycle several times in the minutes that followed. Before my eyes was a passage that sounded a great deal like passages from *The Quality School,* but this wasn't *The Quality School.* It was a "red book." I kept read-ing, and the passages that followed echoed the same similar Glasser princi-ples. I went back and read the pages leading up to the first paragraph that I had stumbled on, and they too reflected the Quality School themes.

It was a beautiful spring morning, with sunshine pouring through my office windows, but I became almost unaware of my surroundings. I was so intent on understanding what I had just read that my vision, my hear-ing, all of my senses, seemed to focus on the book lying in front of me on the desk. I leaned forward and read the passages again. The words were the same. It hadn't been a trick or a misperception on my part. I found myself getting excited. I wanted to share this discovery with someone.

Staff worship began soon thereafter, and I read to the assembled mem-bers what I had found. I wanted to come across as cool and measured, but it was hard to hide my excitement. My colleagues confirmed my feelings, though, as they shared in my excitement. It was a discovery. It was impor-tant to others besides myself. It had been months since that evening when someone had questioned our interest in Glasser's ideas, and at the same time questioned our desire to follow the path of inspiration, yet here before me was an apparent link between the two sources. One source was a respected body of work within the secular world; the other source was a respected body of work within the religious world and, to my mind, inspired.

That morning a spark was ignited in me to find the extent to which the writings of William Glasser and the writings of Ellen White were sim-ilar. Although I had read a number of Glasser's books already, I reread three of his volumes—*The Quality School; The Quality School Teacher;* and *Choice Theory in the Classroom.*[3] Immediately after reading those books, I read three of Ellen White's books whose themes were devoted to the top-ics of education—*Fundamentals of Christian Education; Counsels to Parents, Teachers, and Students Regarding Christian Education;* and *Education.*

As I read these Spirit of Prophecy volumes I underlined everything that compared with, spoke to, or addressed Quality School principles, or, in other words, the ideas of William Glasser. I shouldn't have been amazed, but I was, by the amount and specificity of the similarities. I didn't have to sur-mise and conjecture as I compared the language of one era with that of an-other almost a century later. Instead, the comparisons stood out in bold similarities.

We have all heard the phrase "seeing is believing." My experience with comparing the beliefs of William Glasser with the writings of Ellen White led me to conclude that the reverse also is true. Do you know what I mean when I say that "believing is seeing"? Glasser's ideas somehow triggered a train of thought and understanding, a school view, and even a worldview, that helped me to see what Ellen White had been emphasizing all along. His ideas influenced my beliefs, and those beliefs adjusted the lens of my thinking as I read passages that I had read many times, only to realize that I was being affected by these passages in important new ways.

The principles of psychology and learning that Glasser describes and emphasizes were also described and emphasized by Ellen White. Glasser believes that teachers shouldn't rely on coercion when managing students. Ellen White felt the same way. Glasser believes that students should be "lead-managed" rather than "boss-managed."[4] So did Ellen White. Glasser bases his ideas on what he now calls choice theory, a theory that states that the only person we can control is ourselves, and that rather than being victims of circumstances or events or other people, we are always making choices that we think are best for us. Glasser describes the dangers of external control, or "stimulus-response theory," as he used to call it. Ellen White shared that concern. Glasser believes in the value and importance of relationships.

Every Quality School will be built on a foundation of caring between all who are involved at the school. Mrs. White spoke even more strongly on this need for intentional friendship. Glasser believes that managing students should be based on support, communication, and relationships, instead of punishment. Ellen White emphasized the same principles of management, and then went even further as she wove a deeply spiritual component throughout the tapestry of classroom management. And finally, Glasser describes a curriculum that is based on usefulness and relevance, instead of regurgitation and memory. White stated these points just as strongly.

The chapters that follow will back up my claims that there are significant and profound similarities between these two authors. It has been exciting to see and hear the responses of Adventist educators and parents as they see the comparison for the first time. During presentations, common reactions include stunned but quiet gasps, heads shaking in affirmation of what they are seeing on the screen, and intense concentration as they contemplate how the similarities could be so similar.

One area of note is that as I have shared the Glasser/White correlations with teachers and educational administrators in seminar and workshop settings, I haven't been concerned with whether the examples were striking enough to demand attention, or whether there were enough examples to make the point. Instead, the challenge for me was to pick out the best examples from among the many that existed. I wondered if I had chosen that key phrase or sentence or paragraph that would accurately represent the many there were from which to choose. For me, the exercise of doing the comparative study was not microscopic in nature. In other words, I didn't have to do overly careful, interpretive reading, trying to ferret out the hidden comparisons. I didn't have to gain access to little-known material accumulating dust in some vault somewhere. As I point out in the presentations, it is all "over-the-counter Ellen White." It's material to which we all have access. In most cases the access is as close as our bookshelves at home.

Another point that is incredibly important revolves around the original question that began my search for answers: "Why do we have to go to secular authors when we have our Bibles and the Spirit of Prophecy?" What can we gain from secular opinions? Is attempting to seek insights from secular sources like trying to get water from a dry well—or worse, trying to get water from a poisoned well? The well didn't turn out to be dry or poisonous for me as I began to consider Glasser's ideas. His beliefs and views resonated deep within me and clarified thoughts I had been mulling over for years. Yet Glasser did not develop choice theory through a religious lens. He would say that spirituality was not a part of his thinking at all. So how do we bring the sacred and the secular together? I believe that Ellen White anticipated such a situation when she wrote the following:

"The world has had its great teachers, men of giant intellect and extensive research, men whose utterances have stimulated thought and opened to view vast fields of knowledge; and these men have been honored as guides and benefactors of their race; but there is One who stands higher than they. We can trace the line of the world's teachers as far back as human records extend; but the Light was before them. As the moon and the stars of our solar system shine by the reflected light of the sun, so, as far as their teaching is true, do the world's great thinkers reflect the rays of the Sun of Righteousness. Every gleam of thought, every flash of intellect, is from the Light of the world" (*Education*, pp. 13, 14).

"But there is One who stands higher than they." When I read this passage, I frequently pause over the word "One," with a capital O. It refers to God and how involved He is in our learning, how His inspiration is at work in many ways and in many places of which we are not aware. God continues to be active and influential in the affairs of this planet and desires to communicate to us through those who reflect His thinking. We are too quick to place God in a box of our own making, based on our limited vision and expectations. I think that William Glasser is one of the world's "great teachers," and whether he knows it or not, many of his ideas reflect the rays of the Sun of Righteousness. This book is meant to point out areas in his thinking that seem to be corroborated by Scripture and the Spirit of Prophecy. Each of us can decide whether that is true. Does God work through both spiritual and secular authors and thinkers? Is it possible that in the "thought world" as in the physical world, the rain falls on all of us?

After compiling key examples and statements from both authors, I began to share what I had discovered with colleagues. Their interest and encouragement led to a few small presentations that then led to more presentations to larger numbers of educators. Each time, people would ask for the quotes. I began to give out printed copies of the PowerPoint slides, but I was not totally comfortable with doing so. I am not necessarily supportive of a focus on quotes because such a focus can lead to a narrow perspective that seeks to prove a point or maintain a position. Since I had done the study comparing the two authors, though, I knew that the quotes were not representative of a narrow focus but were indeed representative of larger, obvious themes. If people attended the workshop presentation I felt I could explain these larger themes, which would then help to prevent the problems that come with a narrower focus. The chapters in this book are based on the workshop presentations and are meant to help readers re-create the larger themes that are emphasized. In a number of cases in the chapters that follow I have shared more complete explanations than I have given in the workshop setting.

Before we begin the comparisons I would like to say a little more about William Glasser. Over the past four decades he has been a significant contributor to the fields of behavioral science and education. He is a psychiatrist, but his interests have ranged outside of the traditional field of behavioral science. Early in his career he worked in the Ventura School for Girls. It was while working with these girls that he came to the conclusion that it was the experience of school failure that began the downward spiral of so many men and women who eventually were incarcerated in special schools, juvenile halls, and prisons.[5] Their inability to succeed in the school system had thrust them onto a destructive path, a path that often led to antisocial and dysfunctional behaviors.

Glasser became convinced that the way that schools taught actually created student failure. Schools, he concluded, usually taught irrelevant subject matter, assigned grades based on performances on meaningless rote tests, and relied on coercive strategies to try to make students do the work if they showed too little interest or fell behind. In such an environment, relationships suffered and students swam or sank based on their own resources.

With the knowledge gained from his degree in psychiatry, combined with the insights he acquired as a result of working with and observing people, Glasser developed the principles and concepts that he calls "choice theory." Choice theory contends that the only person we can control is ourselves, and that we in fact choose all of our behaviors. These ideas may sound simple enough, but they fly in the face of how society normally operates. The world believes that people can and even should be controlled externally. Schools certainly believe in external control psychology.

To point out how ineffective external control practices are in schools as well as in homes and workplaces, Glasser has become a prolific author, having written more than 20 books. Educators have found that his books challenge the status quo, yet inspire at the same time. He is a critic of present educational practice, but there is an optimism in his voice. It is obvious that he thinks schools can change for the better, and to that end he has written books that describe the ways that administrators and teachers think and behave in a school in which quality is the goal. These books include *Schools Without Failure, Choice Theory in the Classroom, The Quality School, The Quality School Teacher, Choice Theory,* and *Every Student Can Succeed.* Each one enlarges on previous volumes. Over a time period that spans five decades he has worked to improve his ideas, even making changes in his ideas, but through it all the underlying principles have remained the same.

Finally, I want to say something about Ellen White. Some of you who are reading this book may not be members of the Seventh-day Adventist Church and probably have never heard of her before. Most Seventh-day Adventists regard her as an important figure in the development of our church and recognize her continuing influence. Seventh-day Adventists believe that ever since the Fall of humanity God has worked tirelessly to restore us to our original happy and healthy state. Adventists also believe Jesus when He said, "There are many rooms in my Father's home, and I am going to prepare a place for you. If this were not so, I would tell you plainly. When everything is ready, I will come and get you, so that you will always be with me where I am" (John 14:2, 3, NLT).

Throughout the ages God has spared no effort, even sacrificing His

Son, to redeem His creation. Now, at the close of earth's history, I, along with many other Adventists, believe that God sent a messenger to direct our attention to Scripture and to inspire greater understanding of His character and purpose. I believe Ellen White was that messenger.

Although she was not considered a successful student (third grade was as high as she went in her formal schooling) or even a healthy child, she became one of the most prolific authors in the history of publishing. She wrote more than 50 books and 100,000 pages of manuscripts and is the most translated author in any language. She wrote on topics that included religious thought, healthful living, family relationships, education, temperance, and service. She maintained the spirit of a servant throughout her life and gave God the credit for her productivity. In fact, according to her own testimony and that of eyewitnesses, God communicated to her through visions the ideas that she shared with others.

It is on this point that some, even Seventh-day Adventists, stumble. Did God really communicate with her? If so, does that make her an authority in church members' lives or in church affairs?

Ellen White herself emphasized that there is only one authority and that it can be applied in all areas of life—the Holy Bible, the Word of God. She tried to make clear that anything she said or wrote was intended to point people to the Bible and to strengthen their understanding of Scripture and their faith in God. Never for a second did she want people to think that her writings were meant to take the place of the Bible.

In spite of her efforts and clear communication in this area, some members talked about her more than they talked about Jesus, and quoted her more than they quoted Scripture. It seems that quite a few people from my generation (the baby boomers) were raised in homes in which her writing was used as a coercive tool, which then led some to resent her ideas rather than appreciate them. Whatever the reason, not everyone agrees on the role and authority of Ellen White.

My goal in writing this book has not been to establish her as an authority. I believe her when she says that I first need to go to the Bible. I can say that her writings have meant a lot to me as I have searched for meaning in my own spiritual life. For instance, her five-volume Conflict of the Ages Series helped me to understand the Bible like no other writing I have experienced. At the center of this series is a book entitled *The Desire of Ages* (1898), which describes the life of Jesus and the events and people surrounding His earthly journey that led to the cross. Because of reading what she has written I feel that I know Jesus better and appreciate Him more. For me, there is nothing more important. Beyond that, when it comes to commenting on her level of authority I am an educator, not a theologian. Like the blind man healed by Jesus (John 9), who was then interrogated by those wanting to know who healed him and by what authority he was healed, I can only tell you what I know from my own experience.

The point is that we can view Ellen White in different ways and still gain worthwhile information. We can view her as a special spiritual messenger, which makes this book very special indeed, or we can view her as a writer who lived at the turn of the nineteenth century, a contemporary of John Dewey and Maria Montessori. Either way, comparing what she said to a current educational philosopher—a somewhat radical philosopher at that—is a thought-provoking journey.

It is interesting to compare the school improvement issues of today with the school improvement issues of 100 years ago and see that these issues are eerily identical. One hundred years ago the basic arguments were the same. To what extent should the child accommodate the system, or to what extent should the system accommodate the child? Should learning, by design, appeal to the student, or should the student be forced to learn, regardless of his or her interest? Does memorizing facts constitute learning, or is there a deeper form of learning to which we should aim?

In the field of educational research there is a term called *triangulation*. (The term may be used in other fields as well.) The definition of triangulation includes the idea of multiple forms of overlapping, diverse pieces of evidence and perspectives. In layperson's terms triangulation exists when three or more sources point in the same direction. When this occurs in educational research studies, it increases the credibility of the results.

That is one of the reasons that I feel so strongly about the ideas in this book. It seems to me that three different sources—the Bible, Ellen White, and William Glasser—have each pointed us in the same direction when it comes to how we relate to one another and how we should relate to and educate children and students. They each come at the topic from a different perspective and a different time frame. Yet the underlying truths are present in all three. Could it be that God is so interested in our getting some things right that He sends truth to us in many different packages? Could it be He knows that some of us will listen to one source of truth while ignoring others, and that He is willing to speak to us through the voices to which we will listen? Rather than deciding which "voice" or source to eliminate, maybe we should consider whether or not triangulation is taking place.

A principal approached me about the possibility of my sharing some of the workshop information on Glasser and Ellen White with his school board, but I could tell he was fumbling for the right words. I was an associate superintendent of education in the conference where the school was located, so I knew the makeup of his board—mostly younger professionals. I had worked with this board for more than a year, and I felt they sincerely wanted the school to be the best it could be. I felt that they were willing to consider nontraditional approaches if they thought those approaches made sense.

Still, the principal was groping for words as he at first wondered aloud if I would be interested in sharing the information, but then moments later backpedaled from the idea. I gently prodded him to tell me what he was struggling with; he finally explained that he "didn't think Ellen White would play too well with his board."

I thought about it for a second and then responded that maybe it would be just the opposite from what he feared. They were interested in the latest "best practice, best research" on learning. They wanted to know what the best secular authors had to say about effective teaching practices. Maybe Ellen White would take on a new significance for them if they saw that she spoke to the best in current, cutting-edge educational practice. Maybe if they saw evidence that her views are contemporary they would let her out of the irrelevant historical box in which many have placed her.

I think there are a lot of people who need to see a contemporary Ellen White. The opposite need exists as well. Some are so narrowly focused on Ellen White (a condition that she herself deplored) that they refuse to see truth that comes from any other source. Hopefully, this book will help people with that viewpoint to feel more comfortable with being open to finding truth in a variety of places, even secular sources.

---

[1] "Red books" is a colloquial term used by some members of the Seventh-day Adventist Church to refer to the books written by Ellen White. Many years ago her books were published with red leatherette covers; this led to the term that is used to this day.

[2] Also a term used by members of the Seventh-day Adventist Church to refer to the work and writing of Ellen White.

[3] At the time, the book was entitled *Control Theory in the Classroom,* but Glasser has since changed from using the term *control theory* to *choice theory.* There were no changes in the specifics of control theory or in the principles on which it is based. Glasser just feels that choice theory is more accurate as a title.

[4] *Lead-management* and *boss-management* are terms that Glasser describes in his book *The Quality School.* He credits W. Edwards Deming for influencing him to a great degree in this area, as Deming applied lead-management practices to the workplace setting and achieved higher quality in the process.

[5] The Ventura School for Girls was an institution run by the state of California for the treatment of older adolescent girls. The girls had been committed to the school for offenses ranging from incorrigibility to first-degree murder. The low, one-story, red-brick buildings, surrounded by a high fence and secure against escape, housed approximately 400 girls from all over California. A girl committed by the county to the state for transfer to the Ventura School usually had had several years of supervision by county probation services without success.

CHAPTER 2

Hey!
Where's the Recipe?

"If you want to truly understand something, try to change it."—Kurt Lewin.

"It may be hard for an egg to turn into a bird; it would be a jolly sight harder for it to learn to fly while remaining an egg. We are like eggs at present, and you cannot go on indefinitely being just an ordinary, decent egg. We must be hatched or go bad."—C. S. Lewis.

It's not that I have a problem with what you're saying . . . but . . . it's just that . . . well . . . there are just so many 'save the world' educational solutions out there. You get excited about one of them and a year later the experts are saying something else. I respect your enthusiasm and sincerity, but . . . I just feel that every new thing that comes around really isn't that new. I've seen them before." The 20-year-veteran teacher who made this statement then got a look on his face that as much as said, *OK, what are you going to say to that?*

I think he expected me to argue the points he had made, to defend a professional growth angle, or at least to encourage him to hang in there, but I did none of those. He was right. There are a lot of educational solutions being touted as the answer. These solutions appear in newspaper articles, in columnists' editorials, in political speeches, professional educational journals, in educational research results, in books by experts describing a multitude of models and paradigms and systems and beliefs, and in workshops and seminars by people who live far away from where you live, which therefore qualifies them as experts.

And if that is not enough complication, all of these options are intensified by a constant pressure on schools and educators to improve. I don't know of any other field that has undergone the kind of scrutiny that schooling practices have undergone. School administrators and teachers often experience pressure from district office entities when it comes to controlling student behavior policies and curriculum expectations. Standards and benchmarks may be mandated from above, often without resource support to meet those mandates. At the same time, these administrators and teachers may face an entirely different set of expectations and pressures—often with a significant measure of feeling and passion—from parents. It's a complicated environment, and for the most part the answers aren't obvious.

A picture from "the good ol' days" comes to mind. A horse-drawn wagon slowly approaches the edge of town. The horse is in no hurry, so only a small amount of dust trails off behind the curiously loaded wagon. The driver has been nodding off and dozing for miles, yet now as he enters town his eyes become alert and his senses quicken as he looks for a place to set up his wares. Locals notice his arrival, and a number of them are glad to see him. Others shake their heads in mild disgust and head off to complete whatever errand they were on. He picks his spot and opens the side doors of the wagon to reveal housewares and tools and toys and clothing and—and elixir. "Yes," he says, "it's the elixir of health—guaranteed to cure what ails you." The traveling salesman has come to town, and a small crowd gathers to see what juices or contraptions he's selling now. "Come one, come all," he bellows. "You've got needs, you've got problems, and I've got answers." Even skeptics are swayed by his confidence. A comical picture, we might think now, but is the situation in the field of education that much different?

One of the things that contributed to the success of the traveling salesman of the nineteenth century was the fact that people did have real aches and real pains. Aunt Emma's arthritis was real. The pain was acute. Uncle John's gout was a problem. It debilitated him. Opportunists thrive on opportunity, and for the traveling salesman Aunt Emma and Uncle John spelled OPPORTUNITY in capital letters.

Our needs in education are real as well. Pockets of success are well documented, but as a general rule the system is under attack for producing students that are falling behind in the international marketplace, for demanding little and getting even less in return, for low test scores, low matriculation rates, and low morale. There is within this environment something akin to desperation, something like the drowning person grabbing for the passing tree branch. Educators, like Aunt Emma, are often anxious to try what you've got. Sometimes they are thinking, *What do we have to lose?*

A principal who wanted his school to improve once told me, "If you give me a recipe, I'll follow it." I didn't doubt his sincerity, and I wished I had a recipe to give him; but the fact is that there is no recipe for becoming a quality school. Every community, every school, every staff, and every student body is different, and the roads to success are often unique. Quality is never achieved through checklists, and working with people is always delightfully messier than following step-by-step instructions.

We yearn for life to be simpler. It's not that we want it to be easy—most of us are willing to work hard, to give all of our effort, to come earlier and stay longer. But working longer hours in itself rarely solves the kind of challenges facing our schools today. Solutions for complex problems come from wise effort, not longer hours. The principal who asked for a recipe wasn't afraid of hard work. He just wanted to know what to do first, and then what to do second, and third, and so on.

The teacher frustrated by the multitude of "save the world" educational solutions was, to a significant degree, right. His concern even has a name. It is called the "pendulum effect." Just as a pendulum slowly swings back and forth, coming and going in predictable cycles, so too do educational paradigms and strategies. As another veteran educator put it: "The buzzwords in education today are just repackaged buzzwords from 20 years ago. Wait 20 years and you will see the same stuff again." It sounds a bit cynical, yet there is truth in that view. But simply discounting ideas or new strategies because we have heard them before may not be any better than accepting every new idea that comes along. Because a strategy or belief appears to be a part of the pendulum effect does not mean that it should be eliminated. It may mean just the opposite—the concept might be so good that it won't go away!

Education majors and graduate students in education are reminded of this fact when they take History of Curriculum courses, especially when they read the original writing of prominent thought leaders from the past. John Dewey, considered by many to be the most prominent of American educational philosophers, strongly emphasized during the early part of the 1900s the need for experiential learning and that students create meaning and understanding from those experiences. Those ideas are being emphasized again at the beginning of the twenty-first century. Does that make his ideas wrong or ineffective? Quite the contrary.

There is a danger in making too much of the pendulum. Some educators see the pendulum phenomena as a reason *not* to get involved with any new teaching strategies. They might attend a workshop, but they will often bring a newspaper with them and sit in the back with others who feel as they do, willing to listen to a degree, but having little intention of actually being changed by the information. "Stick with the tried and true" is their mantra, which basically means stick with the familiar.

Traditional methods of instruction may be familiar, but such methods lead to mixed results at best.★ It is true that a percentage of students (Glasser believes less than half) seem to learn in a traditional environment, but many students are left out of the learning or left behind. Schools strive for efficiency with an "assembly line" approach to learning. Unfortunately, people cannot be constructed like cars, television sets, or furniture. In any case the pendulum effect continues to have a profound influence on schools and classrooms. Teaching is demanding and complex, and teachers have little time for retooling or restructuring. But nothing short of restructuring will bring about an environment in which students and teachers thrive.

My passion is that students, teachers, and schools will thrive. Because of that, I have been on the lookout for effective models of instruction and school organization. When I worked in the Pacific Northwest for seven years as a school principal and associate superintendent, I discovered that I was not alone in that quest. There were others wanting to find the components that would be present in an exemplary Adventist school. There were others who shared a conviction that cooperative learning was important. There were others who agreed on the value of Glasser's Quality School model, on Marzano's Dimensions of Learning model, on Kovalik's model of Integrated Thematic Instruction and its emphasis on brain-compatible factors, on Boyer's Basic School model, and on the key ideas of Gallup's Teacher Perceiver interview model, to name a few.

We were engaged in these different models in varying degrees. Some of us read books to get an idea of what the model was trying to do, while others of us attended workshops, and still others received extensive, in-depth training. As a result of my search and my association with other "searchers" I came to an important conclusion—that there are threads of consistency and similarity running through these different-yet-effective learning models. When I really studied the main ideas and beliefs in each of the models, I came to realize that the underlying principles or foundations on which the models were built were similar if not identical. While the models remained just as important and impressive to me, the underlying principles took on even greater importance.

A different metaphor now came to represent educational improvement efforts. Instead of the pendulum and its predictable cycles of futility, a better example would be that of the blindfolded dolphin. My family became annual-pass charter members of Marine World when we relocated to Vallejo, California. We lived 45 minutes away, and our kids were of the age that they really enjoyed the animals and the nature shows. In the whale and dolphin show something took place that fittingly describes the journey of educational reformers or, better said, educational transformers.

The trainer called a dolphin over to the side of the large tank and placed a soft patch over each eye. The patches were made of a foam material and caused no discomfort to the dolphin. The trainer tossed two rings out into the pool, one ring way out to the left and the other way out to the right. He gave the dolphin a signal, and a remarkable thing happened. I did not know this until I attended the show (I must not have been paying attention in tenth-grade biology class), but dolphins are equipped with sonar echo location. Even when blindfolded, they can create an image in their brains based on the returning signals from the pings that they transmit.

From my seat in the large stadium I could see the dolphin turn and then start to head in the general direction of one of the rings. Its path was not a direct path—you could almost see its internal compass homing in on the target. A stronger signal here; slightly weaker there; back this way; no, a little more in this direction; but always headed basically toward that small ring in the large tank. Soon it closed in on the first ring, snagged it on its nose, and then turned to find the second ring, the whole process repeating itself once again. Its pathway to the remaining ring was just as indirect, yet every turn, every correction, brought it closer to its goal.

I believe this is an accurate picture of what we are doing. Educators who seek excellence are like the dolphin—on the alert for effective ideas, and homing in on those principles that will create an exemplary school that is a good place for all students and staff. Rather than the futility of the pendulum, there is a body of knowledge and a body of educators that is more aptly represented by the remarkable ability of the blindfolded dolphin.

This body of knowledge is the focus of this book, especially as it relates to the beliefs and ideas of Ellen White and William Glasser. There are a number of educational theorists and models that appeal to me, but Glasser seems to get to the heart of the matter and explain how people operate, how we attempt to control others (who are similarly attempting to control us), how important relationships are to personal and corporate success, and how we choose all of our behaviors. Only when we begin to understand how people think and operate can we begin to change education strategies and practices effectively.

To help you understand the specific foundation components, I have summarized some of Glasser's key beliefs, which form the basis for what he now calls choice theory. We will look at each of these beliefs more closely throughout the book, but as we embark on this journey together I thought it would be good if you could begin to consider these ideas early on. I summarize Glasser's ideas as follows:

- We choose all of our behaviors based on what we think will be best for us. We can't control our physiology or emotions directly, but we can choose our thoughts and actions.

- External control wrecks relationships. Whether in family settings at home, learning settings in the school, or business settings in the workplace, external control puts a wedge between people and ultimately lowers the quality of friendships and productivity.

- Coercion (another way of saying external control), whether through negative reminders, threats, and punishments, or through the use of positive rewards as a way to manipulate behavior, leads to poorer-quality work rather than better work. Coercive practices, especially negative ones such as punishment, also lead to adversarial relationships.

- External control theory, or stimulus-response theory (as it can also be called), is wrong. It is the opposite of choice theory. B. F. Skinner believed that people could be trained or controlled into behaving or performing in certain ways, even though people are tremendously different than the pigeons with which he usually worked. Behaviorism says that people are motivated and even controlled from external forces; choice theory says that all of our motivation comes from within. This is a very significant difference with very big implications!

- People who want to employ the principles of choice theory will become lead-managers rather than boss-managers. Lead-managers foster positive relationships, lead by example and invitation, are clear in their expectations, yet supportive during their completion, and attempt to stay clear of threats and "power moves."

- Genuine friendships, intentional "liking" relationships, are a part of successful schools and workplaces. Whether it is staff with fellow staff, or staff with students, or students with fellow students, a high priority is placed on supportive relationships.

- Management, or school discipline, is built within an atmosphere of trust and support. A key component of good classroom management is schoolwork and lessons being based on relevance and student interest. Students who have a good relationship with their teacher and who are engaged in the learning have no interest in misbehavior. When mistakes occur, though, effective management will rely on discussion, solutions, and redemptive management rather than lecture and punishment. Redemptive management allows the student to "restore what has been broken."

- Schoolwork focuses on relevance and usefulness and always ends in mastery and understanding. Superficial work, sloppy thinking, and marginal performance on projects and tests are not options.

- Student learning increases when students are effectively organized into student learning teams, or cooperative groups. This format will not be used exclusively in a Quality School, but it will be used a lot. Students need to verbalize what they are thinking, to explain to others what they know, to engage in defending and improving their ideas. They especially need to learn to work with others and to recognize the potential of the group. Each student has insights, skills, and gifts, into which a skilled learning team can tap.

These summarize the key components of Glasser's ideas. Yet to be honest, several of these components also reflect the ideas of other theorists and their models and approaches. If you are familiar with one of these other approaches, you may have come to this conclusion already. *Hey,* you might be thinking, *This sounds a lot like what I learned from so and so,* or *This is exactly like what I experienced at that workshop I went to last spring.* It wouldn't surprise me at all if that were the case. In fact, that has been my experience.

There are other excellent approaches from which we need to learn. What has helped me organize these different approaches, though (the human brain, through patterns and associations, constantly searches for ways to create meaning), is my view that choice theory, as far as recent secular models go, is really the umbrella under which other effective models can gather. Glasser and choice theory describe a paradigm, or view of life, that is distinctive.

If one appreciates the ideas that make choice theory distinctive, then other approaches begin to catch our attention. These other approaches do not compete with Glasser's ideas. Instead, they complement or enlarge them. For instance, because Glasser has helped me to realize that the curriculum needs to be relevant and useful, I am drawn to Susan Kovalik's Integrated Thematic Instruction model, which I think shows teachers how to put Glasser's ideas into practice. For the same reason I am drawn to Roger Taylor and his integrated instructional approach.

These other models (and there are many more like them) are effective, and seeking to understand them and to implement them represents good use of our time. Districts and schools pay large sums of money for trainers to in-service teachers in many of these different approaches. My thinking is that such training may be good, but without understanding the foundation on which these approaches sit, our efforts will result in mixed success. Good things come from these training sessions, but one seems to always feel that the situation is a bit precarious. A solid foundation will strengthen in-service efforts in other models as well. Choice theory is the best current secular source I know that helps in our understanding of the foundation.

Principals and teachers lead pressured, busy lives. They live and work in a special realm that few appreciate. Teaching is highly complex, made more so by the varying needs and preferences of students and parents. This complexity is further complicated by societal expectations. Change is demanded, yet it seems that whenever change is attempted it is met with skepticism, censure, and little support. This kind of environment leads to the belief that if change is going to happen, it needs to be quick.

Educators may be open to try new things, but the steps to change must be clearly laid out. That is why certain workshops have such popular appeal. Testimonials of teachers who have attended these workshops go something like "I got lots of ideas that I could put to use right away!" or "The workshop was really well organized. It gave me the steps—like one, two, three." Oh, that lasting change were that easy. But it isn't.

Permanent change begins with a change of heart. And heart change does not occur according to a schedule, a checklist, a mandate, or a workshop. I have likened the change that Ellen White, writing at the turn of the past century, and William Glasser, writing at the turn of this century, promotes to that of a journey. The principles of life and learning that they describe alight on us slowly, almost imperceptibly, as we reflect on our own experience through the filter of their ideas. We think on these things privately before we think aloud to others. We practice noncoercive lead-management privately before we implement these strategies publicly. We come to believe in choice theory personally before we put it to use professionally. We want a quick recipe, not a long journey, but the changes that White and Glasser describe are too profound for a recipe to cover. Instead of simply providing ideas on how to teach, they give us ideas on how to live. Because permanent change begins with the heart.

---

* When I use the term *traditional methods* I am referring to an approach that is teacher-centered, linear, and rote, and in which coverage of material is more important than depth or understanding. Little value is placed on the need for relevance or usefulness or in wrapping the learning around student interests. Little emphasis is placed on how brains actually learn through discovery and how the learner creates meaning from his or her experience rather than meaning being poured into his or her head like lemonade into a glass. Almost no emphasis is placed on mastery. Under a traditional grading system the students have the option of not mastering the material. Seat time is more important than understanding.

CHAPTER 3

The Power of Choice

"The strongest principle of growth lies in human choice."—*George Eliot.*
"The ideal aim of education is creation of power of self-control."—*John Dewey.*

Understanding the power of choice is of infinite importance. We were created with the power of individuality, with the freedom to think and to act. Since humanity's creation, though, this freedom has been under attack. To some, freedom is a threat or problem that must be controlled. Freedom, these would say, is a nuisance that leads to trouble. Others, though, see this freedom or power as essential and have gone to great lengths to preserve it, even to the point of shedding their own blood in its defense.

This freedom, the power of choice, is the issue in a great cosmic, universal controversy that has lasted for millennia. Even though incredible effort and resources have been devoted to eradicating this freedom, it has been preserved. Choice survives. Although the battle has raged for centuries, it is plain now that this freedom will last forever, longer than the present great controversy, which is fast coming to an end. As a human race we began our existence with the power to choose, and that power has been saved in the face of incredible odds. Those who understand this power will ultimately join a universe of beings who live according to this same principle.

Sound a little over the top? a little melodramatic? Maybe, but it is all true. And while the power of choice is of cosmic consequence, for those of us on this planet it is also the stuff of daily life. We know it's there, and most of the time we would agree that we have it, but that something is missing. We have choices, but somehow we lack the power to follow through. Religion is supposed to enhance our power to choose, to make it stronger; but often it seems to have the opposite effect.

The cosmic struggle is played out in each of us every day. The apostle Paul was frustrated by this struggle so much that he expressed that he couldn't make himself do right. "I want to," he said, "but I can't. When I want to do good, I don't. And when I try not to do wrong, I do it anyway" (Rom. 7:18, 19, NLT).

As parents and teachers we deal with this struggle on a regular basis too, not just in our own lives but also in the lives of our children and our students. Parents struggle with how to manage their children, how to get them to do what they should do, and how firmly they should attempt to make them behave. Teachers struggle with not just one or two children but with a whole classroom of students. They wrestle with the same questions as parents. They wonder how to get students to do what they should do. And if the students don't do it, what should be the response?

In answer to these questions, parents and teachers succumb to a force or pressure that truly is remarkable. It's what this chapter is about, actually. Because if, in spite of cosmic implications and the fact that we are created with the power to think and to choose, kids aren't doing what they are supposed to do, parents and teachers go into a special mode. It is the I-am-going-to-make-you-do-this mode. The remarkable pressure, then, is the urge to use force. It is at the heart of the whole arena concerning making and coercing and compelling and complying. It doesn't work that well in the everyday scheme of things, but we continue to use the strategy anyway. (Some of you might be saying, "Hey, I can make my kids do what I want them to do," but in this you miss the point. Keep reading.)

What is the source of this force's staying power? Is it human nature to want to control and coerce others? Do we have a need to control others because of how we were treated when we were growing up? Or can it actually be traced back to something deeper, something that involves the great controversy?

John Dewey (1859-1952), earlier referred to as probably the most influential of all American philosophers, saw the matter plainly enough. He wrote, "The history of educational theory is marked by opposition between the idea that education is development from within and that it is formation from without; that it is based on natural endowments and that education is a process of overcoming natural inclination and substituting in its place habits acquired under external pressure."

The approaches and strategies of schools in the twentieth and twenty-first centuries have continued this basic debate. Is learning something that is invited and inspired from within or is it imposed from without? The record, along with the personal experience of almost everyone reading these pages, shows that schools and homes have depended on strategies of imposition. Adults know what is best, and kids need to comply. (Some of you may be asking, "Are we just supposed to let kids do whatever they want to do?" No. But keep reading.) Parents and teachers yearn for their charges to do well, to be successful, and to treat others well in the process. We yearn for these outcomes so deeply that when students aren't heading toward success as we define success, we feel it our responsibility, even our obligation, to see that they change direction.

Feeling a strong desire for our children or our students to be successful is not the problem, though. The problem lies in how we deal with students (or anyone of any age, for that matter) when they deviate from the path we think they should be following. We often do know what is best for kids, but it is how we tell them and show them what is best that makes all the difference in the world—and in the world to come.

The issue of external control and coercion needs to be considered on both the practical and spiritual levels. While coercive strategies on a practical level (daily life here on earth) hurts relationships and hinders productivity, it is its impact on the spiritual level (our deeper happiness and eternal future) that is the most important.

Consider the strategies of the two forms of government in the universe between which we have to choose. In the first, God has placed a high premium on our freedom. In fact, it is nonnegotiable with Him. So important is freedom, and His created beings having the ability to choose, that He risked everything to ensure its preservation. So important is freedom that Jesus gave His life to guarantee it forever. When Lucifer began his rebellion, God could have destroyed him, and further, could have erased from every memory that he had ever existed. But such an act would have robbed us of the ability to make decisions based on the weight of evidence. We would have been mere automatons.

In his proposed form of government, Satan has revealed his strategies. Rather than give men choices he wishes to remove the ability to choose. He wants nothing less than to enslave and trap. Nothing satisfies him more than for one of God's free-will human beings to be addicted to a life-eroding, life-destroying substance or practice. He dangles the guise of freedom in front of men only to lure them to dungeons of unhappiness. This is why

God proclaims through Isaiah that "captives will be released and prisoners will be freed" (Isa. 61:1, NLT). God's government cannot tolerate entrapment or coercion of any kind.

On the practical level we wonder what kind of management works best with people. Teachers especially want to know how to manage students. We wonder how coercive we should be to make them do what we want them to do. (We actually wonder the same thing with everyone we deal with, not just our children or our students. Spouses often receive our special coercive strategies.)

But it is the implications on the spiritual, eternal level that should really cause us to pause and think about what we are doing. If there is one thing we should want to get right, it is an accurate understanding of the character of God. And if God is noncoercive, what are the implications for me as a parent or a teacher? For instance, what does this passage from *The Desire of Ages* have to do with my practical daily strategies of living and relating to others? "In the work of redemption there is no compulsion. No external force is employed. Under the influence of the Spirit of God, man is left free to choose whom he will serve" (p. 466).

Albert sat in a room just down the hall from the principal's office. The staff used the room for worships in the morning, but Albert wasn't thinking worshipful thoughts at the moment. He had just been escorted to the room, also used as a time-out room when students needed to calm down or get control, by his teacher. Albert had "blown up" because his teacher, Mr. Creswell, had moved him to another part of the classroom in the hope that Albert would quit distracting others and begin to work on his assignment.

Albert was a new student to the school and, in his own words, "wasn't going to take any ——— off of anybody!" Albert was Hispanic by blood, but he was American in attitude. His parents had immigrated from Mexico, but Albert had been born in the United States. The streets of central California were his home as far as he was concerned. It was his grandmother who wanted him to be in a Christian school. At first Albert had wanted that too. But his old ways, especially his temper, sometimes got the best of him. Now he sat waiting for the principal, or whoever was going to deal with him.

Albert was a "project" the school had accepted, and for the most part Albert was hanging in there. This time, though, Albert had crossed a significant line. He had yelled at his teacher in front of the other students and included the use of inappropriate language. He had also slammed the door on the way out of the classroom. Albert was basically a sensitive kid, but he would be ready for a fight as soon as someone walked into the room.

Over the past year the staff had been studying the principles of the Quality School. During the summer they had received training in choice theory. They had listened to the presenter give examples of how to work with upset students, and everyone had agreed with how the example scenarios had been handled. Now Albert was providing them with their own test case.

Stan Creswell had received the training too, and was willing and able to continue to work with Albert. After bringing Albert to the worship room, he stuck his head in the principal's office and briefly described what had happened.

Brad Thompson had been the principal at the school for five years but had been learning about choice theory for only the past two years. He did not consider himself an expert by any stretch of the imagination, yet he had slowly and consistently led the rest of the staff toward a better understanding of choice theory principles. He wanted staff members to try to put the principles into practice, but he also expected the same from himself. "Do you want me to handle it?" Brad asked.

"Actually," Stan replied, "I think that might be good for a couple of reasons. One, I won't have a break until after fourth period, and two, Albert and I have worked through a couple of situations already this year and it might be good for him if he experienced someone else. If you can't do it, I understand."

"It won't be a problem. I think what I will do is attempt to help him get to the point where he understands what happened and what he can do to prevent it in the future. If he wants to come back to the classroom, could you take it from there, or would you like me to take it further than that?"

"If you could help him up to that point I can do the rest." Creswell felt a sense of appreciation at being able to work with his principal and was thankful that he had experienced the choice theory training along with the teachers.

"Let's check with each other after school and compare notes." Brad also felt a sense of appreciation at having teachers like Stan on the staff.

The thought crossed Brad's mind that this is where the rubber meets the road. *What were those key points the presenter had made again?* he questioned himself. A specific plan didn't materialize in his mind, though, and he realized that he was just going to have to wade into the matter and rely on his beliefs and his training. He said a silent prayer and walked down the hallway to meet with Albert.

As he entered the room Albert looked up at him with a wary, defensive look. "So, what brings you to the staff worship room, Albert?" the principal began.

You have probably walked down such a hallway yourself. I know that I have. We enter the room, and our eyes lock onto the student's eyes. It is easy to see that the student is angry. Soon we find ourselves in a no-win situation, in which eventually we use our position and power as teacher or principal (parents experience similar situations at home) and tell the kid what his punishment will be.

We leave feeling upset too. Working with nonproductive or unresponsive students can be a frustrating task, especially if parents and teachers think that they need to *make* a student behave in a certain way.

Before we hear how Brad Thompson actually worked with Albert, maybe it would be good to consider Albert's situation through the eyes of a principal who believed in a traditional approach, an approach based on telling rather than inviting, threats rather than guidance. Let's pick up the scenario from where we left it earlier.

"So, what brings you to the staff worship room, Albert?" the principal began. Albert averted his eyes and was now looking at the table. When he remained quiet, the principal continued. "I understand there was a problem in your classroom. Do you want to tell me about it?"

Albert's head remained lowered. "Not really."

"Do you want to tell me how you are feeling?" He felt he was trying to accommodate the student.

"No, not really." The kid had clammed up.

The principal started to become slightly frustrated. "Well, I think we need to talk about it." Albert still offered nothing, so the principal continued. "What set you off? Do you think you have a reason for what you did?" The principal continued looking at Albert, but Albert continued looking down at the table. "Do you think you might be able to look at me when we are talking?" Albert slowly lifted his eyes, but they were full of disgust. "Well?" the principal demanded.

"You want to talk about feelings? OK, I feel like that teacher stinks!"

His principal gave Albert a knowing look. "You want to play it that way? You think that is going to help the situation?"

"Whatever," Albert mumbled.

"Look, tough guy, you are out of that classroom until you get your act together. In fact, at this rate you may find yourself out of the school." The principal was now looking at Albert with an expression that conveyed, *I'm not going to put up with this.*

"I don't want to go back in there anyway." Albert didn't want to put up with things, either.

"Albert, you better shape up, or things are going to get ugly. I am not kidding. This is serious." Albert wasn't responding as he should have, and the principal was groping for the words that would have the necessary impact. He was about ready to threaten him with expulsion. The principal left the room feeling that the conversation had gone nowhere. He was convinced that Albert had a bad attitude and that he had better change that attitude or else.

The interaction above is not unusual. As adults we use looks, sometimes subtle, sometimes obvious, to convey our anger or our disgust. Our words can be used as weapons of intimidation or threat. We try to think of ways to make others, especially children and students, do what we want. In implementing such an approach, we forget that human beings are motivated from within rather than from without. We also forget the tremendous power that human beings, including our children and students, have to make choices. Of course, what we want is something totally different than the interaction described above. There are reasons these interactions don't go well, though, and Glasser describes those reasons at length. He has assembled these ideas into what he calls choice theory.

Choice theory is the foundation on which Glasser builds his education theories and practice. Choice theory can be outlined in several concise statements, but while the statements may be short the implications are very deep. The implications made a difference in why the above scenario between the principal and Albert did not go well. Consider the following axioms of choice theory (not a complete list) taken from chapter 13 of Glasser's *Choice Theory*.

- The only person whose behavior we can control is our own.
- All we can give or get from other people is information.
- We are driven by five genetic needs: survival, love and belonging, power, freedom, and fun. These needs have to be satisfied. They can be delayed but not denied. We can help others, but we can never satisfy anyone else's needs, only our own.
- All behavior is total behavior and is made up of four inseparable components: acting, thinking, feeling, and physiology.
- All total behavior is designated by verbs, usually infinitives and gerunds, and named by the component that is most recognizable. For example, "I am choosing to depress" or "I am depressing" instead of I am suffering from depression or I am depressed.

✐ All total behavior is chosen, but we have direct control over only the acting and thinking components. We can, however, control our feelings and physiology indirectly through how we choose to act and think.

Glasser uses the picture of an automobile to better explain this idea of total behavior. The steering wheel represents our wants. The engine of the car represents our needs. It is those five genetic needs that each of us has in varying degrees that drive us or that provide the interest and energy for our choices.

The four tires of the car represent the different components of our behavior—thinking, acting, feeling, and physiology. It is significant that the two rear tires represent feeling and physiology, while the two front tires represent thinking and acting.

Glasser explains that while all behavior is total behavior, the only part of our behavior that we can directly control is our thinking and our acting. When we drive a car the only tires we directly control are the two front tires, yet the back tires follow the front tires' lead. Where the front tires go, the rear tires follow. Glasser says it is the same with our total behavior. We do not have direct control over our feelings, but we can choose the way we think and act. As the rear tires follow the front tires, so too will our feelings follow the lead of our thinking and action. We may not have direct control over our emotions and physiology, but we do indirectly.

You may have questions about the components of what Glasser calls total behavior; if so, I invite you to consider the following. Think about the physiology of behavior for a moment. When I was a principal in a small town, it was difficult to go anywhere without bumping into people I knew. Many of the people had students in my school. Most of the time bumping into people was fine, but occasionally it wasn't so fine.

I can remember heading down the hill to get a few groceries, only to spot a certain model and make of car parked in front of the store. I immediately recognized the car and realized that it belonged to a certain family with which the school was having a difficult time. Almost simultaneously with my brain's identifying the car came a clenching feeling in my stomach. It wasn't a conscious thought—it was an automatic reflex. I could not intentionally control that clenching feeling. I entered the store, worried about whom I would bump into or what I would do if the person acted angrily toward me. The physiology component was definitely a part of my behavior, but it was a part that I could not purposely control at that moment.

Our feelings are similar to our physiology. We know they are there.

We feel them strongly. They have a powerful effect on our outlook. They are sometimes pleasurable, but on the flip side they can be very painful. At times it seems that they can control us, hold us captive and keep us down. All of which makes our feelings, at times, extremely frustrating. We try to control our ups and downs, we try to control a strong reaction, we don't want to be depressed, but we seem incapable of changing our feelings. And indeed, we aren't capable of directly controlling our feelings.

Because of this, Glasser offers some good advice when it comes to working with our children or our students. "When I discuss counseling nonproductive students, it does no good for the teacher to focus on the students' feelings or physiology. . . . Focus as much as possible on the behavioral components the students can change—their actions and thoughts" (*The Quality School,* p. 86).

We need to remember that our students are no different than we are when it comes to what we can and can't directly control. It is certainly easy to focus on a student's feelings, as that component often seems to be the most obvious; but when we do this, we are entering a no-win situation. When students are asked to describe their feelings, or when they are accused of feeling a certain way, their natural reaction is not only to describe them but also to defend them. By defending his or her feelings, a student seeks to blame someone or something else for how he or she felt and behaved.

When we blame others, the focus is actually on their behavior, not ours. Beyond that, a focus on feelings, is not productive because we rarely understand why we feel the way we do. There just are no simple explanations to what causes our feelings. I once heard a friend, a psychiatrist, actually attempt to explain this thing called feelings and the reasons we do certain things. "There is the reason we tell others," he began. "There is the reason we tell our spouses. There is the reason we tell ourselves. And then," he paused here for effect, "there is the real reason." There is probably a lot of truth in that.

While we cannot directly control our physiological responses or our feelings, Glasser says that we can choose our thoughts and our actions. This is a powerful statement that offers not only power but freedom as well. People don't have to be bound by their reactive behaviors. They can choose how they will respond. As I thought about the idea that we can choose our thoughts and our actions, it hit me that this is a very Christian way to think. Ellen White corroborates Glasser's premise that thinking is not only a part of our total behavior; it can also be under our control.

"Right thinking lies at the foundation of right action" (*Fundamentals of Christian Education*, p. 248).

"No one but yourself can control your thoughts" (*Our High Calling*, p. 112).

"The actual discipline of life is made up of the little things. The training of the thoughts is essential" (*Mind, Character, and Personality*, vol. 2, p. 656).

"If the thoughts are wrong, the feelings will be wrong" (*Testimonies for the Church*, vol. 5, p. 310).

The mentality of victimhood is so prevalent. Students are ready to blame others for their mistakes. Rather than take responsibility for their behavior, children of all ages point to unfair circumstances beyond their control as the cause of their poor choices. Unfortunately, this kind of behavior is not limited to children. In fact, our children and students learned the "blame game" from us, the significant adults in their lives. Victimhood is so common that many of us would disagree that we can control our thinking. "Aren't we just victims of the thoughts that come into our heads?" some ask. Ellen White and William Glasser state that our thinking is the result of choices we make. This is how God designed us. This is what it means to be free.

The way in which we give our students choices takes on special significance within this context. How we coach them in knowing how to make a choice, and in helping them to realize that they are not victims of circumstance or trapped in a bad situation is really the key to their present as well as their future. Choice theory is about empowerment and responsibility.

"You yourselves are responsible for the kind of character you build" (*Fundamentals of Christian Education*, p. 245).

Do we, even as adults, understand the scope of this responsibility? Do we realize the power and ability we have to make choices? It is easy to feel that we are the victims of circumstances, or that we simply react to life as it comes, whatever that may be. But choice theory and the Spirit of Prophecy describe a much more powerful and proactive way to live.

It is interesting to compare the choice theory model to other models of motivation and behavior. Chapter 6 will cover this in greater detail, but a few words should be said here regarding the model of behaviorism. Glasser makes a point of stating just how different his model is from the principles that drive behaviorism:

"It is important that we recognize that this theory [choice] is almost the exact opposite of the traditional stimulus-response theory [behaviorism] that has led us to where we are now" (*Control Theory*, p. 7).

In what way is choice theory the exact opposite of stimulus-response? Think about this. It's important. Behaviorism is based on the belief that people can be motivated and even controlled by external stimuli. Choice theory contends that we are motivated from within. Glasser helps us understand behaviorism by describing the key beliefs of stimulus-response, or external control, as he now calls it.

Key Beliefs of External Control

First belief: I answer a ringing phone, open the door to a doorbell, stop at a red light, or do countless other things because I am responding to a simple external signal.

Second belief: I can make other people do what I want them to do, even if they do not want to do it. And other people can control how I think, act, and feel.

Third belief: It is right, it is even my moral obligation, to ridicule, threaten, or punish those who don't do what I tell them to do or even reward them if it will get them to do what I want.

The ideas behind these beliefs are probably very familiar to you. Most of us probably think that we are experiencing them every day. External stimuli or circumstances do control or motivate us, don't they? Glasser says no, and his explanation has life-changing potential.

"The foundation of these beliefs, that we are externally motivated, is wrong. For example, we do not answer a phone because it rings; we answer it because we want to. You may argue, 'If I don't answer the phone because it rings, then what's the purpose of the ring? I certainly don't go around answering phones that aren't ringing.' The ring does have a purpose, but it is not to make you answer. It is to give you information, to tell you that someone out there wants to talk to someone here. The ringing of the phone, and all else we perceive from the outside world, is information. But information is not control. Choice theory explains that stimuli, in the sense that they can consistently control a human being to make a specific choice, do not exist. Whatever behavior we choose is generated inside our brains. We are, as all living creatures are, internally motivated" (*Choice Theory,* pp. 16, 17).

Glasser tells the story of a friend of his who was visiting Las Vegas. One time when his friend was entering his hotel room, another person slipped into the room behind him before the door could latch. When his friend turned around, he was confronted by a man pointing a gun at him and demanding that he turn over his wallet. At this point the friend did something that I don't recommend. He said, "Look, I'll give you my cash, but I'm not giving you my wallet."

The thief must have been frustrated at this and responded with "What do you mean, you're not giving me the wallet? I have a gun here!" He waved the gun for effect. Guns are usually excellent external controllers.

"I'll give you my cash, like I said, but I don't want to mess with my credit cards and have to deal with canceling them and all that." In the face of a gun being pointed at him, the position he took on the wallet seems extremely ill advised; yet he was acting on something that was important to him.

The thief was incredulous, apparently so much that he took the cash and left without the wallet. Of course, the story could have ended tragically, but that isn't the point. The point is that the friend's internal thinking overruled the external circumstances. The thief gave him information—*I want your wallet, and I can hurt you or kill you with this gun if you do not give it to me.* The information was indeed a powerful stimulus, but it did not force the friend to hand over the wallet.

As you read this story maybe you started thinking of similar examples. One such story is that of the three Hebrew youth standing before King Nebuchadnezzar (Dan. 3). A great golden statue had been erected and the people called together to celebrate and affirm the leadership of their king. It was quite an affair. Many powerful people and dignitaries from around the kingdom were there. It was a visual spectacle. And the full orchestra was there, too, adding incredible sound to the incredible sights.

At one point in the ceremony the orchestra played and everyone present bowed down to the image. What a sight it must have been—except that everyone wasn't bowing. Among the prostrate crowd there were three bodies still upright. You know the story. The three men were brought before Nebuchadnezzar, at which point the "information sharing" begans." Similar to the thief in Las Vegas who proclaimed, "Hey, I've got a gun," Nebuchadnezzar proclaimed, "Hey, I've got these furnaces!" As he gave this information men were stoking the furnaces even hotter. Bow down or burn.

Certain that Meshach, Shadrach, and Abednego had only momentarily lost their senses, the king offered them another chance. *You probably just misunderstood,* he thought to himself. *Now, let's behave correctly and just get on with this as planned.* But the youth, polite through it all, and in the midst of incredible external control—the anger of the king, the pressure of the crowd, and the super-hot furnaces near enough for them to feel the heat—

firmly stated that they did not need another chance. Their God was powerful enough to save them, but even if He did not save them they would not bow to the image. Amazing! There was something inside of them (or internally motivating them, as Glasser would say) that was more important than the external controllers with which they were being threatened.

Glasser contends that we do what we do because we choose to. A ringing phone doesn't make us pick it up. If someone answers it, it is because he or she chooses to answer it. Some people seem to answer the phone reflexively. The phone rings, and they jump to answer it, almost in a panic. Others are just the opposite. They seem not to care whether or not it is answered. Maybe they have an answering machine and will check the messages later. Maybe they are expecting an unpleasant phone call and don't want to risk picking up the receiver. The fact is, we answer the ringing phone or don't answer it for reasons that are pertinent to us.

The same can be said about a traffic signal. Does the red light make us stop? While we might be tempted to say that it does, we now realize that the light doesn't make us stop. It gives us information that it is our turn to stop, thus allowing other cars to cross the intersection. What we do with that information is up to us. Almost every time I come to a red light I choose to stop because I see it in my best interest and in the interest of others for me to do so. I don't want to get in an accident and risk injury. Nor do I want to hassle with insurance companies. And I don't want to receive the ire of fellow human beings for acting like a jerk behind the wheel of a car.

I say "almost every time" because there are circumstances in which I will disregard red lights. Late one night I came to a signal and sat there as it went through its changes. Instead of turning green for the left turn lane the signal seemed to have skipped me, leaving me sitting there staring at a red light. *This light is dumb,* I thought to myself. There was not another car around for as far as I could see in any direction, and there I was held captive by this "dumb" red light. I decided I'd risk it and turned left anyway. The light was giving me information, but I chose to disregard the information.

Another time, I was visiting family, along with a number of friends, in the mountains to the east of Redding, California. At close to midnight one evening I was told that I needed to get one of the young men staying with us to the emergency room immediately. Although 21 years of age he had recently had a tonsillectomy, and that evening he had started to bleed in the back of his throat. This, I was told, was very serious, even life-threatening, and must be treated quickly.

Several of us got into the car and headed to Redding. At this point I was feeling as if I had an excellent reason to disregard speed limits and traffic signals. I think we averaged about 95 miles an hour on the way to the hospital, and I lost track of how many red lights I disregarded. (Some of you are thinking that my speed and intersection behavior were stupid, but that isn't the point, even though I think you are probably right.) The speed limit signs and traffic signals were giving me information (that I almost always respect and adhere to), but I was motivated by something else that I felt was more important.

It is this ability to choose that Glasser continually emphasizes. We can control someone, but that someone is us. We can't control others, and others can't control us. Or said in another way, we can control others or others can control us only to the degree that we choose to let each other do so. The bottom line, though, is that *"we can control only what we do"* *(The Quality School,* p. 44; italics supplied).

Choice theory is based on this principle. It is a statement made up of only seven words, yet it is packed with truth that can change your life and change the way you relate to others.

Teachers often spend a great deal of time and energy trying to control their students. They operate under the belief that they need to make their students behave, or to *make* them do their assignments, or to *make* them treat each other well. It is a draining experience. Yet we are reminded that "we can control only what we do."

Marriage partners also fall into the pattern of wanting to control the behavior of their spouses. Tremendous amounts of stress and grief are experienced by one or both partners as they struggle to control or manipulate each other externally. This pattern has destroyed so many marriages and created so much havoc in homes that it is amazing we haven't realized it before now and done something about it. Instead, we go on believing that people can be externally controlled and that we can make another person do what we want them to do.

It would be difficult to overstate the importance of people's ability to make choices. Effective schools intentionally include choices as a part of the learning process. Effective homes begin early in children's lives to teach them about making choices, including experiencing the results of both good and bad decisions.

But the value of choice-making goes even deeper than this. The responsibility we as Christians have to make choices is a spiritual issue as well. It is easy to think that we are sometimes the victims of circumstances or temptations. Life deals us certain cards, and we react. But choice theory doesn't give us any room for such excuses. And neither does the Spirit of Prophecy. The following quote really struck me. Like Glasser, Ellen White states that what we think is under our direct control. Drawing again on the picture of the car, we see that it is plain that she would place the behavioral component of thinking as one of the two front tires: "It is within the power of everyone to choose the topics that shall occupy the thoughts and shape the character" (*Education,* p. 127).

What does this mean? Can we really have control over what we think? Does this include thoughts of disappointment and discouragement and depression? What about anger and resentment? Thoughts of vengeance or competitiveness? Does this statement include lustful thoughts, too? If it is true that we can "choose the topics that shall occupy the thoughts and shape the character," then incredible possibilities are available to us. Rather than our thoughts controlling us, or even influencing us, we can choose the thoughts on which our minds dwell. Imagine how lives could change if this principle were accepted and implemented.

And imagine the impact that this principle would have on children as their experiences lead them into adulthood. It is one thing to give students the power of choice; it is quite another to help them understand the *power* of choice. "Every child should understand the true force of the will. The will is the governing power in the nature of man, the power of decision, or choice" (*ibid.,* p. 289).

I am confident that Adventist educators would, if asked, wholeheartedly agree with the above quote. It is hard to argue with. It, along with others that emphasize the need for children to have a sense of self-government, reminds us that schools must be a place where students' choices and wills are exercised.

Yet I ask you, How are schools teaching students to be self-governed and self-directed? In traditional, teacher-centered classrooms students have very little input as to what happens in their room during the day. Teachers usually design and implement the behavior guidelines of the room. They decide when students are misbehaving, and then decide what happens to them afterward. The focus is on compliance rather than guidance in making choices. Academically the story is the same. Students are given teacher-planned assignments, which the teacher evaluates after they are completed. Teachers often struggle to limit the choices students may have, and even to eliminate choice at all. It is so much simpler when there are fewer or no choices with which to deal.

"There is urgent need of schools in which the youth may be trained to habits of self-control" (*Fundamentals of Christian Education,* p. 64).

How do students learn self-control? As much as we may not like to admit it, students learn to have self-control as they are given chances to make choices and then live with the results. As with everyone else on this planet, we learn by making mistakes. This is a hard thing to do within a school setting. Parents and teachers do not want their children making mistakes.

"The object of discipline is the training of the child for self-government. He should be taught self-reliance and self-control" (*Education,* p. 287).

It seems to me that many educators and parents misunderstand the issues surrounding self-control, self-government, or self-reliance. It is not a universal problem, because I do see some teachers and schools putting into practice the very thing that Glasser and Ellen White are talking about. But for the most part, adults seem to misunderstand the process of children and students learning to make choices. This misunderstanding affects the way we work with students, as well as how we work with ourselves. Unfortunately, our success rate at controlling others or ourselves doesn't appear to be very good.

I think our misunderstanding exists for several reasons. First, we were probably reared with the very techniques and tactics that we are now questioning. It is very hard to change habits and beliefs that have been ingrained since childhood. Second, societal pressures have pushed us in this direction too. There is a strong desire to believe that we can control others; if we can figure out what carrot or what stick to use when working with our children or our colleagues, we will be able to get what we want.

Third—and maybe this is the most important reason of all—this misunderstanding reflects how we feel about God and the way He operates with us. To come to understand what self-government means to us as educators, we will have to figure out how God relates to us. And when I say "what it means to us as educators," I am not thinking about how we work with students. I am thinking about how we work with ourselves. I am thinking about our individual integrity. I am thinking about how we behave when no one is looking. I am thinking about our—or should I say my—personal honesty.

"The highest evidence of nobility in a Christian is self-control" (*The Desire of Ages,* p. 301).

This really is the goal. And because this is the goal, because self-control is the highest evidence of our nobility as Christians, getting students to behave well is not enough. Having them under control is not enough. Their good behavior must be based on their choices, not on my coercion.

Their acting appropriately should occur because they see the sense of it, not because I am making them behave that way. And remember that this is the goal—this thing called self-control—because God set it up this way. The Trinity cooperated in saving us by preserving our power to choose. They not only paid the penalty for our rebellion, They continue to act on our behalf through the quiet influence of the Spirit, providing strength, comfort, courage, patience, and love.

I received an unsigned letter; other than the postmark on the envelope from a large city, there was no indication of who had sent it to me. I don't think the author would mind my sharing it with you. It said: "I don't suppose very many teachers share with you their struggles over integrity issues. It is so embarrassing not to lead a consistently honest personal life. Each of the topics you covered was interesting, but it was the section on self-control that seemed to captivate me and terrorize me at the same time. No offense to your presentation ability, but I think the Holy Spirit was the one doing the captivating and maybe even the terrorizing.

"I have been struggling with this idea of where temptation comes from and why I could not repel even the slightest attack. I felt powerless, and for the most part—at least as far as my actual behavior would have indicated—I had given up. And then you shared that stuff on our power to choose, including that quote on how we have the power to choose the topics to think about. It seemed to fill me with hope. Since then I find myself thinking on those ideas, and I am coming to the conclusion that Glasser and White were right.

"I should add that I believe any of these efforts on my part, or any thoughts that are good, are from the Holy Spirit. But I somehow feel more able to understand and grasp that power now. Somehow, understanding my role has made a difference. Like the tax collector in Luke 18, I really feel that I deserve none of God's favor, but I am comforted by the many promises of Scripture. And I am committed to my students understanding this gift we call choice. Where have we been for so long?"

Maybe the more important question is not Where have we been? but Where are we going with this truth? If Glasser and Ellen White are right, how will it change the way we do business? How will it change the way we think as individuals? Is it possible for Adventist homes and schools to be places where students learn to make choices, and where they learn to really take responsibility for their actions and even their thinking?

At the start of this chapter we met Albert Orozco, an eighth grader who had been asked to leave his classroom and who now found himself in the staff worship room just down the hall from the principal's office. We considered how the conversation between the principal and Albert might have gone if the principal had approached Albert using traditional reward/punishment language and strategies. But now let's consider what can happen when a different strategy is used. How might the interaction go if the principal wanted to place the responsibility for Albert's behavior on Albert, yet offered caring and support in the process? Brad Thompson had been practicing the principles of choice theory for almost two years and was ready to work with Albert. Let's pick up the same scenario once again . . .

As Mr. Thompson entered the room Albert looked up at him with a wary, defensive look. "So, what brings you to the staff worship room, Albert?" the principal began.

Albert averted his eyes and was now looking at the table. When Albert remained quiet the principal continued. "I understand there was a problem in your classroom. Do you want to tell me about it?"

Albert's head remained lowered. "Not really."

"Well, I'm not sure exactly what happened, but it doesn't sound as though you're very happy." Albert still remained quiet, head lowered. Brad's voice remained calm, even upbeat. "I'm interested in talking with you about your being happier in school." He started to move toward the door, but stopped before heading out of the room. "You may need time to think about things. Let me know when you want to talk." That said, he turned to walk out of the room.

"I don't need time to think!" Albert was still upset, but his head was up and he was trying to glare at his principal, who seemed friendly and not upset at all. "This is dumb! I can't believe this! How long do I have to be in this room, anyway?"

"As far as time goes, I'm not sure. I just want this thing resolved." Albert made a disgusted grunt, but the principal didn't react to it. "I want you back in your classroom, and I'm willing to help you if you want my help. Let me know." Again he turned to leave.

"Hey, you can't just leave me here!"

"Look, I don't particularly want you in here, either. But you seem upset and unwilling to talk. I am willing to help, but not if you are unwilling to work on it too." Brad's voice was friendly, yet firm.

"Look, I messed up!" Albert almost shouted. "What do you want?"

Brad stepped back into the room and looked at Albert. He didn't say anything right away, but his eyes locked on Albert's until Albert looked away. "I want you to do well here. I want you to know that we care about you." Albert made some small grunting noise. "I think you'll do better if you're happier."

"Yeah . . . well, I'm not happy."

"I can see that. But you asked me what I want, and that's what I want." Brad wondered if he was saying the right things. Albert continued looking down at his shoes and didn't seem interested in talking further. "I'll check with you in a little bit. I'm not in a hurry." Again Brad turned to head to his office.

"So I have to stay in here." Albert's tone was changing a bit. His voice was quieter, the anger not quite so sharp.

"For now, yes. I'll be back in a while." And with that he turned and walked out.

Brad had gotten Albert's assignment for the class he was missing and the books needed to complete the assignment, but when he returned to check on how Albert was doing it was plain that Albert had not spent any time on it. Albert was still upset, but Brad could tell that he was calmer than before. Time helps in that way. Albert mustered up some more indignation and asked, "Look, what do I have to do to get out of here?" Although the room was pleasant enough, to Albert it was a bit boring.

"Why don't you tell me what happened?" Brad had talked some more with Mr. Creswell and also with several students who had witnessed the incident, but he wanted to hear Albert's version of the event too.

Albert sighed, but then he began to share what had happened. "Creswell was getting on my case and he wouldn't let up, and next thing I know I'm in here." He glanced at his principal, almost expecting him to return with some sarcastic remark regarding his version of the incident.

No sarcasm, though. Instead Brad asked, "That's it? That's what happened?"

"Well . . . I said some things I probably shouldn't have said." Albert glanced up again.

"That's it?"

"I slammed the door pretty good when I went out of the room." Albert's body language was a confused mix of "I'm tough; leave me alone" and "I can't believe I did what I just described."

"H'mm . . ." Brad thought quietly. "Do you want to go back to the classroom?"

"No," Albert replied, but his answer lacked the intense conviction that had attended most of what he had said up to that point.

"Well, I guess you can make that choice." Brad noticed a slight look of surprise on Albert's face when he said that. "What will it mean to you if you make that decision?"

Albert looked at his principal now, almost trying to see if this guy was for real or not. "I don't know, man."

"That's a pretty big decision, though. What do you think it would mean for you?"

"It would mean I would go to another school . . . maybe a public school or something." Albert was trying to stay tough, but anyone could have picked up on his discomfort at having the focus placed back on his choices.

"You can do that, but how would that help you?"

"Look, man, I don't know how it will help me! I just want out of here!"

"I understand, Albert. Sometimes it is hard to know everything that we are thinking or feeling." Brad felt for Albert at this point. He could see a kid that had been too much on his own. "You know, I am willing to help you get to where you want to go, even if that is to another school, but I really want you here."

"I can't deal with Creswell. He's got it in for me."

Brad felt a tinge of wanting to jump to his colleague's defense, but replied matter-of-factly, "What happened that has you thinking Mr. Creswell has it in for you?"

Albert rolled his eyes and shook his head from side to side. "The guy won't leave me alone. I can't visit with my friends or anything. The guy is obsessed."

"You're talking about visiting during math time?" Brad asked.

"Hey, it's not like I'm making a big scene or anything. I mean, the guy is obsessed."

"So if Mr. Creswell wants students to work on math during math class, you think that he is obsessed?" Brad studied Albert for a clue to his reaction on this point. "What did he say to you when he wanted you to do your work?"

"He said, 'Work on this assignment.'"

"And that is unreasonable to you?" Brad knew that Stan Creswell had asked Albert to work on his assignment in a different way than Albert had just mimicked, but he felt that wasn't the real point at the moment.

"Look, sometimes I like to do my work at home."

"How is your grade in the class so far?" Brad knew that Albert's grade was in the high D range.

"I don't know . . . It's probably not that good."

"So how is your strategy of not working in class and doing the work at home . . . how is that working . . . do you think?"

"Look, I don't care about math." Albert sounded a bit exasperated.

"And you want Mr. Creswell and your classmates not to care about math too?" Brad was starting to feel that Albert was not really serious about resolving anything.

"Yeah, I want them all not to care about math. That would be great." Albert had a smart-aleck look on his face.

"Well, even without the yelling at your teacher and the slamming of the door, it doesn't sound as if you want to be in the class, or that the class would do much good for you. I don't think I can do a lot for you at the moment." Just then the school secretary stuck her head in the door and said that Brad had a phone call from a person that Brad had been trying to reach for most of the week, and wondered if he wanted to take the call or not. "Yes, I'll take it," he replied, but he looked at Albert as he said it.

"You're going to leave me in here again?" Albert whined. "I thought we were fixing this thing."

"Fixing it?" Brad repeated. "So far you have told me that you don't want to be in this school, or in Mr. Creswell's classroom, and that you don't want to buckle down and try to learn math. What's fixed?" Brad looked at Albert again. "I need to take this call. You might want to consider doing the schoolwork . . . the assignment there." He turned and headed to his office.

Alone in the room, Albert found himself in what, for him, was a strange situation. He was trying to be mad, to keep his intensity up, but it was difficult. He had messed up; he knew that. But his principal was not in his face, not blaming him or threatening him or even bargaining with him. *This is weird,* he thought to himself, but deep within there was a spark of hope, too. He actually looked at the sheet that described his assignment and picked up his book and turned to the pages to be read. He kept thinking, though, about how he would get out of this mess and how his grandmother would feel when she found out.

When Brad returned after the phone call and after he had been shown the furnace room by the maintenance man, where it was explained that unless a very important part was replaced now it would result in a more costly repair later, and after he had checked on how the substitute teacher was doing in the fourth grade, he pointed out to Albert that "I want you here, but I can't make you want to be here." He paused here, searching for the right words. "Anyway, the decision to go to another school is too big to make quickly. I think you should think about it for a few days at least . . ."

"Look," Albert interrupted, "I've been thinking . . . and I really think I should probably go to school here . . . you know . . . with my grand-mother and all. It would really mess her up . . . you know, like disappoint her . . . you know."

"Yes, yes, I know. She would be disappointed." Brad had a feeling that bringing up the subject of Grandma was more of a way for Albert to save face, but that was all right with him. "That's good. I'm glad you feel that way. So you think you should stay, then?"

Albert looked thoughtful, like he was thinking deeply. "Yeah, I think so."

"Excellent! You know, that is a big part of the solution to this thing. When you want to be here, things tend to go a lot better."

"So what do I have to do? How do I get back into the classroom?" There was a gentle sincerity in Albert's voice for the first time since the whole thing started.

"Well," Brad thought aloud, "it seems that you need to come up with a plan for things to go better in the classroom. What is your responsibility for staying in control of yourself?"

Albert's countenance fell a bit. "That sounds complicated."

"Sometimes it does feel hard, but it is an important part of your doing well in the future."

Albert then came up with what he thought was a great compromise. "Can't you just punish me or something?"

"You think that if I punish you now it will keep you from getting upset or angry in the future?" Brad was really starting to see how punish-ment-oriented even students are.

Albert thought for little bit and then replied, "No, probably not. Punishment has never made me stop doing what I wanted to do."

"So that's my challenge. Why would I punish a student if it really didn't work?"

Albert was at a loss, but finally suggested, "Because that's what princi-pals do?"

"That is what some principals do, and that is even what I have done in the past, but I am tired of solutions that don't work. If I could punish angry behavior out of you, I would probably be tempted to try, but as you said, it doesn't work. This is something you have to solve."

"I don't know where to start. Creswell is going to be so mad at me."

"What happened wasn't good. It affected people. You know, when someone is angry, it affects others. You know what I am saying?" Brad wanted Albert to understand what he had done, but more important, to fill him with hope.

"Yes."

"You might be surprised, but Mr. Creswell believes in you."

Albert paused. "Yeah, I kind of know that. But sometimes he makes me so mad."

"Your plan won't really work if it focuses on anyone else. The only person you can be responsible for is you. You are the only person you can control."

"But I can't help it . . ."

"If you think that you can't help the way you act, then you won't. But I know that you can. I'm positive you can control the way you act." Brad thought he saw a glimmer of confidence or something in Albert's eye.

"I don't know how to make a plan." Albert wasn't whining. He truly didn't know how to make a plan.

"Let me ask you this. When this incident took place, were you being the person you want to be?" Albert didn't answer, but Brad remained quiet. It was important for the ball to stay in Albert's court.

After a long silence Albert said, "No, I wasn't. I lost my temper and made a fool of myself."

"So what would you do differently?"

"I would maybe try to do some work . . . maybe. Or maybe just sit quietly . . . without talking to Tomas or Jordan . . . maybe."

"You think it is that simple? That would do it?"

Albert looked at his principal without really knowing what to say.

"Maybe that would do it," Brad continued. "I don't know. It could work maybe. I'm just thinking that you and Mr. Creswell probably need to compare notes a bit. I think you need to feel that you understand each other better."

"That couldn't hurt."

"Would you be willing to talk with him?"

"Yes, but like I said before, I don't think he is going to want to visit with me. I messed up, man."

"Well, that will be up to him. He will have to make that choice."

Albert just shook his head. "So . . . the plan?"

"You and Mr. Creswell will have to settle on the plan. He and I want students in his room that are willing to cooperate and make efforts to do some quality work. If you want to be in his room, I am sure that you and he can work out the details."

"Don't I need to make things right?"

"What do you mean?"

"You know . . . like apologize or something."

"Personally, when I say something to another person that is hurtful, I like to make it right. It's usually not an easy thing to do, but I feel better after I do it."

"Yeah."

"I think it would be good for you to make it right with Mr. Creswell, but you can handle that when you think it is best. Can the three of us get together and talk about the plan? Would you like my help on that?"

"Yeah, that would be good."

The Albert scenario is just one example of an educator trying to work through a student's misbehavior in a way that places the responsibility for the behavior on the person doing the behaving. It is not an example of a perfect scenario. I don't know that perfection exists in some of the difficult situations in which we sometimes find ourselves. Things could have been done differently in subtle or obvious ways. The principal could have had Albert write out the events, he could have made a bigger deal out of it, he could have suspended him from school until it was resolved, rather than the modified in-school suspension that was described. The teacher could have handled the whole thing. And on and on . . .

If you think it could have been done differently, you're right. But the differences are not as important as the ultimate goal—to help students learn to be responsible for themselves, including their thinking, their feeling, and their actions.

It's about self-control. It has been about self-control since the Garden of Eden. Everything depends on our understanding of the freedom God gives us. This chapter began by recounting how God created us as individuals and the lengths to which He has gone to preserve our power to make freewill choices. In one of the most elegant and revealing passages in the Spirit of Prophecy, Ellen White describes God's goal for men and women, for you and for me, and for our children and students. The passage has to do with how we teach, but it also has to do with how we interact with one another, and especially how we manage or "control" students. God does not seek mere compliance, but instead desires obedience based on understanding, and commitment based on choice.

"Every human being, created in the image of God, is endowed with a power akin to that of the Creator—individuality, power to think and to do. The men in whom this power is developed are the men who bear responsibilities, who are leaders in enterprise, and who influence character. It is the work of true education to develop this power, to train the youth to be thinkers, and not mere reflectors of other men's thought. Instead of confining their study to that which men have said or written, let students be directed to the sources of truth, to the vast fields opened for research in nature and revelation. Let them contemplate the great facts of duty and destiny, and the mind will expand and strengthen. Instead of educated weaklings, institutions of learning may send forth men strong to think and to act, men who are masters and not slaves of circumstances, men who possess breadth of mind, clearness of thought, and the courage of their convictions" (*Education,* pp. 17, 18).

"Strong to think and to act." "Masters and not slaves to circumstances." "Courage of conviction." If these are attributes that we want our children and students to have, then we have to ask if our present strategies of motivation and management will lead to such strength or if they will lead to "educated weaklings." On the one hand we act as conscience and discipliner for the students in our charge, while on the other hand we seek to strengthen students' consciences and empower them with self-management. On the one we limit choices, while on the other we expand them.

This chapter is about the *power* of choice. It's about the incredible spiritual implications regarding this *power*. It's about how Adventist homes and schools can either improve and develop this *power* or erode and possibly eliminate it. It's about parents, principals, and teachers first possessing this *power* themselves.

CHAPTER 4

Being and Becoming

"Be the change that you want to see in the world."—Gandhi.

"Well, the options seem pretty clear to me," he said. He had a way of carving and sanding ideas down to their essential elements. "Do we change the learning to fit students, or do we change students to fit the learning?"—Workshop attendee.

The event that morning was a defining moment. Later, it would be seen as one of many such moments in the young leader's career. For the men who were there, who saw what happened and were a part of the event, it became one of the memories that forever reminded them of who they were and what they could be. As the team drifted toward shore, their navigational and directional equipment totally destroyed in the storm, the morning dawn was transforming the black of night into subtle shades of light that slowly dimmed the brilliance of the stars until the light said goodbye to the night and the sun erupted on the eastern horizon.

It was hard to believe, after what they had just experienced, that the day promised to be so glorious. The temperature of the air was cool but not uncomfortable, and the sky was blue for as far as the eye could see. It seemed strange, too, that this morning calm and beauty was the backdrop for a war and all that war brings with it.

As the keel slid onto the sand and gravel of the shore, each team member felt a mix of emotions. Their behaviors were a mix too. A few talked lightly, almost joking, while others were quiet and relieved. What they each had in common, though, was a seriousness that lay deep in their eyes.

Battle zones tend to promote a seriousness of purpose. Only a few of the team had ever been on this shore before, yet it was common knowledge that terrorists had struck several times in this area.

As the team stepped onto the sand, their senses were switched onto "wary." Eyes scanned every direction, especially the wide trail that came down to the beach and the bushes and rock formations on each side of it. Their ears strained to pick up sounds that reveal the presence of someone they should prepare for—a twig snapping under a person's or animal's weight, a pebble dislodged from the bank above the trail. Even their sense of smell was on high alert.

Their leader moved up the beach as though he knew where he was going. Two of the team members secured the vessel onshore and then caught up to the group as it headed up the trail to who knows where. Maybe their wariness was misplaced after all. The day was indeed glorious. The green of spring with its many accompanying colors stretched into the distant hills and met the blue sky, which seemed bluer and deeper and wider than usual. Several team members visited quietly as they walked, their wariness lessening as they moved away from the water and the terror of the night before.

The attack came without warning. Caught by surprise, team members bumped into each other as they fled, while they tried to determine from which direction the attack was coming. There was screaming and noises impossible to describe, noises that sounded more animal than human, noises that seemed to be coming from more than one direction, echoing off near rocks and bushes, piercing the air, their ears, and their hearts. Instinctively they ran, and upon actually seeing what was doing the screaming, they broke into a sprint back down the trail.

What they saw looked like a nightmare rather than real life on this glorious day. At least two creatures, apparently half man and half animal, were attacking them from each side, with all the ferocity and passion that can be imagined. Each of the team members thought his life was over. They knew they couldn't fight such creatures, and if they were half animal they certainly couldn't outrun them, either. They ran back down the trail, with the terrifying expectation that something would grab them from behind and drag them down in a violent heap. They ran on sheer adrenaline until even their adrenaline ran out. Their lungs could not keep up with the demand, and their legs, without fuel, grew heavy and stumbling.

As they neared the shoreline, the pain in their lungs and their legs overruled their fear, and they stopped, expecting the worst, but the worst did not come. Only the sound of their heavy panting could be heard, with the faint lapping of the small waves. When they turned one by one to see where their attackers were, their eyes took in that moment, that defining moment.

They thought for certain that all of them had fled the attack, but all of them had not fled. One was missing from their group, and he now stood, alone, before the creatures that had moments before lunged from the rocks bent on destruction and death. It was an amazing picture, a forever memory. Three forms, two half crouching, yearning to kill, and one, erect, calm, with no fear, wanting to heal. Time seemed to stop. There was no sound. The eyes of those by the shore, the escapers, squinted to focus on everything that was happening back up the trail.

Later that night as they lay on their bed rolls reviewing the day, they each tried to rationalize their behavior, tried to explain or defend their fear, but there was no way around it. They had fled in terror and left their leader, their point man, in danger. How had he remained calm when the attack came? How did he know he could handle it? How could he be so fearless? How could he look into the jaws of hell and not flinch?

And at the evening meal, when each of them expected him to chide them or scold them, or just be silently disgusted with their fear, there was none of that. Instead, he said they could be fearless too. In fact, he said that each of them would come to be fearless, and that they would change the world. As he talked with such confidence, they looked at him with tears in their eyes, tears of embarrassment at their quick retreat, and tears of love for someone who believed in them even when they did not believe in themselves.

Years later, when they were on their own and facing the gates of hell, facing attacks and even death, they remembered that morning and the fact that He, too, had faced down hell, that He had faced it first. If He could do it, so could they.

∞

Leadership like that of Jesus with His disciples (Matt. 8:28-34), leadership that inspires others to do their best, to be fearless, and to do what is right regardless of the outcome, is a special legacy in an age when we see so few examples of true leadership. When we work with children and students, we have a very special opportunity to model that kind of leadership.

Schools are special places. Teachers take students, with their past and all its challenges, and introduce them to the present with its excitement and frustration, while all along pointing them to the future with its promise and responsibility. Students are the future. How do they become ready to not only take care of themselves but to take care of each other, and contribute to this earth we call home?

To a great extent, young people become ready for the future through the leadership of significant adults around them. All the time, through many circumstances, they watch us. Children value themselves as we value them. They come to value others as we value others. They believe in their own ability as we believe in their ability. Their optimism mirrors our optimism. As parents and teachers we are leaders in the truest sense, yet often we forget our role as leaders.

Much has been written about leadership over the years. Companies want to increase profits, and good leadership is essential. Much has been written about leadership in other areas, too, such as schools and even homes. People seem to crave descriptions of effective management techniques. We want ideas on what to do or not to do. We have a situation in mind and wonder what a good teacher or parent would do in the particular case we are thinking of. We want to do the right thing. Whether we are presidents of big companies, supervisors of a department, principals of a school, teachers, or parents, we want to do the right thing. Good management is needed whenever and wherever people need to work together and get things done. Places that need to work together and get things done pretty much describe homes and schools.

When it comes to manager behavior, Glasser introduces us to two terms that are a key to our understanding. Those terms are *lead-management* and *boss-management*. He believes strongly that if quality is going to be achieved, either in industry or in classrooms or in homes, managers, teachers, and parents will have to understand and implement lead-management. Teachers, for instance, who are lead-managers treat students very differently than a traditional boss-manager.

If it is our goal that students actually want to come to school, and once there, actually want to do their best work, then they will have to feel an ownership of the work that needs to be done. They will have to feel that they are a part of the planning, and even a part of the evaluation process. To create this kind of environment, teachers will have to understand lead-management. Let's look at some descriptors of a lead-managed classroom:

1. The teacher makes a constant effort to fit the work to the needs of the students.

This difference should not be underestimated. In a traditional classroom, material is presented to students much as a fender is added to a car on an assembly line. In other words, the students must adapt themselves to the material, which in effect is nonnegotiable.

The lead-manager, on the other hand, believes there is more than one way to accomplish understanding and competence and is willing to help students achieve quality in multiple ways. Teachers skilled in Multiple Intelligence approaches, for instance, are very comfortable with this idea. In fact, once teachers begin to experience a classroom where students can complete an assignment in one of several ways, or where student needs are accommodated, they say they will never go back to the assembly-line methods.

2. The teacher is a facilitator that creates a noncoercive, non-adversarial atmosphere.

The lead-manager teacher understands the value of positive relationships with students. Instead of punishing the misbehavior out of students, lead-managers seek to understand what is causing the problem in the first place, while enlisting the "problem student's" help in coming up with a solution. When teachers simply punish, it always leads to the student and teacher being adversaries. When that happens, the teacher jeopardizes his or her ability to influence or reach the student.

It is natural for teachers to assume the more traditional role as boss in the classroom. In the boss role the teachers take responsibility for everyone's behavior, both behavioral and academic. They become police, detective, and judge, as well as arbitrator, medic, and records keeper. This can be a tiring role for the teacher, a role the students are all too happy to let the teacher assume.

3. The teacher shows students how to evaluate their own work.

This is one area in which we educators have a long way to go. The system is very teacher-centered when it comes to grades and evaluation. Traditionally, the kids do the work and the teacher tells them how well they did on it. The result of this setup is that students seem very content to do shoddy work. Spelling errors are frequent, organization is lacking, and neatness is rarely evident. Teachers threaten students with poor grades if assignments aren't completed or if they are turned in late, but this does not seem to make a difference. Students do not feel ownership of their work, and therefore do not feel responsible to do their best.

I have heard it said that the only evaluation worth anything is self-evaluation. I have thought about that statement a lot and have come to the conclusion that it is pretty much right. The ultimate goal is not that teachers be good judges of their students' performance; rather a teacher's goal should be that students learn to evaluate their own work and to judge their own product's effectiveness. Rather than having students dependent on our opinions, we must slowly wean them from relying on our judgments of what they produce or create.

4. The teacher shows or models how work is to be done, and listens to student input as to how it could be done better.

The lead-manager is willing to be a leader, not a pusher. A leader leads; a pusher bosses. A leader models what he or she is trying to get across, whereas a boss tells students what to do and how to do it. Nowhere is lead-management more important than in the area of spiritual issues. Values and beliefs can be talked about in Bible class, but the life a teacher lives will speak volumes more than the most eloquent Bible lectures and discussions. If a teacher desires the classroom to be a community in which students care for one another, then that teacher must demonstrate how a caring person behaves. In academics teachers can give one assignment after another, and can grade papers night after night, but unless they have shared their own enthusiasm for learning, the students will only be going through the motions. I heard of a principal who took the sign down from his office door that read "Principal's Office" and replaced it with one that read "Head Learner." That really is what we must portray to our students, that teachers and students are in the learning business together.

These lead-management descriptions can easily be applied to the home setting, too. Classrooms are basically large families. What is said in regard to one can often be applied to the other. Parents, like teachers, need to attempt to fit the expectations to the needs and skills of the child. As much as possible, parents need to see life through the eyes of their children and, where appropriate, make accommodations. Lead-manager parents do everything they can to keep the home setting from becoming adversarial and coercive. They value relationships and recognize the power in connections between family members.

Like classroom evaluations, homes can benefit greatly as children apply self-evaluation strategies to their responsibilities and chores. Homes, too, benefit when parents not only model what they want their children to do but also seek input from their children as to how things can be done better. The issues at home are very similar to those of the classroom.

It's Whom You Know

Ellen White understood the pillars of lead-management. She understood the importance of modeling and example, because she knew how important it is for students to have adults around them who will demonstrate what love and respect and courage and patience are all about. The following statement is probably the best one-sentence description of lead-management that I have come across. It has changed me.

"Let it never be forgotten that the teacher must be what he desires his pupils to *become*" (*Fundamentals of Christian Education,* p. 58).

Back up and read it again. Study it. Write it on a 3" x 5" card and place it where you will frequently see it. It could very well change you the way it changed me. Because now, when I find myself getting a little upset over how a kid is behaving or what a kid is or isn't doing, this sentence scrolls across my mind.

If my own teenager has been too long in front of the television or is watching something that I don't fully approve of and I am about to tell him how I feel about that (with a certain disgusted tone that is probably hard for me to hide), I find myself thinking, *Have I been what I want him to be?* When I am about to lecture him on some issue I ask myself, *Have you been what you want him to become?* All too often I have to answer that I have not been what I want of him. It is so much better if, instead of simply telling him to shut off the television and go find something else to do, I say, "Let's do something together."

This statement also reveals that Ellen White goes so much deeper than other educational writers on this point. With her it isn't so much what you do as much as who you are. This is important.

We need to realize that what we do and what we say spring from who we are. And who we are is dependent on the Person we know. This is why our relationship with Jesus is so important. As we come to know Him better, as He literally becomes our hero, we admire Him more and more and desire to be like Him. His wisdom, His patience, His unconditional caring, begin to become a part of our behavior.

Students see through a fake. Of course, as adults we do too. While there is something a little pathetic about actions that aren't genuine, there is something very powerful about actions that are genuine. When teachers truly are being what they want their students to become, the atmosphere takes on something special. There is an honesty and a caring that is noticeable.

Accepting the role of a model to young people is a heavy responsibility. Many adults seem to shrink from this role or deny it. Charles Barkley, who at the time was an all-star forward for the Houston Rockets basketball team, did commercials in which he emphasized that he "was not a role model. That's the parents' job." But Barkley was wrong. He and other athletes are indeed role models, whether they like it or not.

The bad attitudes that are often seen in professional sports, the bad-mouthing and trash talk, the fighting, the disrespect for officials, and the disregard for coaches and authority in general have all been copied at the junior levels. Kids watch the significant adults in their lives, whether they are on the television screen or in their living room, and they slowly become like the models on which they focus. This same phenomenon is true with teachers. We are role models, not just by how we teach or how well we know our subject matter, but by how we live. Students know where our hearts are.

"If you are called to be a teacher, you are called to be a learner also" (*Counsels to Parents, Teachers, and Students,* p. 199).

The above statement reflects how a lead-manager thinks. Learning is not so much an obligation as an opportunity and a privilege. Learning is an adventure to be enjoyed. The lead-manager loves learning so much that it would be impossible not to "infect" his or her pupils with this same love.

"The object of education is to prepare the young to educate themselves throughout their lives" (Robert Maynard Hutchins).

This really is our object. Our goal is to turn kids on to learning so that even when we are not present they will continue to see learning as in their best interest, and will see learning as enjoyable. Sir Walter Scott once said, "All men who have turned out worth anything have had the chief hand in their own education." Instead of that happening by accident, we need to intentionally prepare students for taking hold of their own learning.

This is where lead-managers are so effective. First, a lead-manager exudes his or her own love of learning. Second, he or she is constantly looking for ways to turn more responsibility over to the students. A lead-manager discusses potential topics for learning before settling on what exactly to teach; he or she works with kids individually as they choose specific areas on which to focus; he or she reviews with them what an excellent assignment looks like and gets students' input as to what they think an excellent assignment would be.

One teacher shared the following: "I chose to be a biology teacher because of the influence of my academy biology teacher. Actually, I started out as a premed student, but as I got closer to making a final career decision, I realized I really wanted to teach. I wanted to be a part of creating the kind of classroom that my teacher had created for me." When I asked her just what had been created, she explained, "When I entered that class-room, I entered a place where learning was important. We all felt that our ideas were valued, that we were dealing with important issues and that our opinions counted. There was a feeling in that room that anything could happen. Maybe we would come up with some cure for a terrible disease, or discover some insect that had never been seen before.

"There was never busywork. All our assignments were more like pro-jects. I remember one assignment had us studying the impact of a devel-opment plan in our community to tear up a 'green area' with a stream running through it and replace it with a strip mall. I did everything from taking water samples in the stream to identifying the different types of life forms and animals that populated the area. I was amazed that I had become so interested in scat samples. I took photographs; I took surveys in the local neighborhoods; I did the math on what a strip mall would actually do for the area, and in the end I had put together a sizable notebook.

"Other students were working on the same assignment, although each of us seemed to attack it from a different angle. I remember how mean-ingful it was for me to listen to small-group and class discussions on our strategies and progress. The thing I will never forget is our teacher arrang-ing with the city council for several of us to present our findings. I was never so scared and yet so determined in my life.

"It has been 15 years since that council meeting, but when I am back home, I still drive by that 'green area.' It's still green to this day. My point is that our teacher made learning relevant, because it was relevant to her. If a particular assignment seemed tough, we knew she would be out in front, that she would be as muddy as the rest of us, or that she would be there in front of the town council with us. That is what I want to be to my students. I want to show them the excitement of learning, and that each of us can make a difference."

"The great aim of the teacher should be the perfecting of Christian character in himself and in his students" (*Counsels to Parents, Teachers, and Students*, p. 68).

I usually didn't have a problem focusing on my students' weaknesses and on the need for them to be perfect. My problem was that I forgot to start with me. Of all the projects that lead-managers must make a priority, their own spiritual walk is the most important. This really is the essence of lead-management. And again, this goes beyond Glasser. The most impor-tant lead-managing that can be done is to reveal to students who our best friend is. We all have heroes. And we all know who each other's heroes are. Do the students see Jesus, our hero, in us?

Another teacher shared a significant memory from his academy days, a memory from something that happened during a physical education class. "Several of the students had been involved in horseplay the day before, and our teacher had let one of the guys have it pretty good. I didn't hear exactly what was said by the teacher, but we all could tell that he wasn't pleased. I guess he was pretty disgusted.

"Anyway, the next day we all lined up for record as usual, and our teacher comes out and starts talking kind of quietly. I still remember his words. He talked about how he had had a hard time sleeping the night before, and said that he had come to the conclusion that he had been a jerk when he had let Ryan have it. The gym got real quiet at this point. He said that he thought the world of each of us and that he always wanted to treat us with respect. Quieter still. He said that he had gotten upset and that that hadn't been called for. Yes, some of us had deserved to be spoken to, he explained, but not in the way he had gone about it.

"One of the guys tried to say, 'Hey, Coach, we were the ones with the problem,' but Coach agreed only to a small degree. 'Yes, some of you had a problem,' he allowed, 'but I ended up with the bigger problem. I acted like Moses yesterday, when he struck the rock. I was angry and I took it out on you.'

"The gym was so quiet. I had never heard it so quiet. 'I have apologized to Ray,' he went on, 'and I appreciate his forgiving me, but the rest of you were present too, and I want to apologize to you as well. I'm sorry.'

"Just a few seconds went by before several voices said, 'It's all right, Coach; no problem.'

"I had never experienced anything like that before. It struck me that my coach was not making excuses, because he sure could have. Those guys acted up more often than not, and had driven several teachers to uncharacteristic displays. I was also struck by how affected we all were by what he had done. The four guys who had acted up were especially affected. Coach modeled something to me about God that day." He ended by asking me, "Is that the kind of thing you are talking about in this lead-management thing?"

Such stories bring out the potential of what can happen when a teacher seeks to be a leader and not a boss. Lead-manager teachers put themselves in the place of the students and struggle to do what is best for them.

A lead-manager tries to see things through his or her students' eyes.

Such a teacher seeks to understand where a student is coming from, what has contributed to a student's problem or challenge, and how to help that student overcome that challenge. When we as teachers and principals take this approach with students, or even with each other, we are said to have empathy. Empathy is one of the most important attitudes we can bring to a relationship. A teacher that exudes empathy is an important resource to students who are looking for someone they can feel comfortable with, someone they can trust. Empathy is the beginning of how we demonstrate compassion. Empathy allows us to break out of our egocentric worlds, our tiny bubbles of concern, and experience the tremendous stories of resolve and courage and sadness and cruelty all around us.

Let's look at this from another angle. I came upon an interesting quote recently that is an example, maybe in an unexpected way, of how a lead-manager thinks.

"The system of grading is sometimes a hindrance to the pupil's real progress. Some pupils are slow at first, and the teacher of these youth needs to exercise great patience. But these pupils may after a short time learn so rapidly as to astonish him. Others may appear to be very brilliant, but time may show that they have blossomed too suddenly. The system of confining children rigidly to grades is not wise" (*Counsels to Parents, Teachers, and Students,* p. 177).

The traditional system of grade levels was originally created for its factory-like efficiency, not because students would learn better. Yet that factory model is now viewed by some as if it was part of some sacred, untouchable, educational institution. The lead-manager looks at the system and asks, "Is this good for kids?" Ellen White, one of the most student-centered educational writers I have read, saw that our artificial grade levels have nothing to do with a student's abilities and readiness to learn. A lead-manager will look at it the same way.

A little aside here: It is interesting that throughout this century the majority of Seventh-day Adventist schools have been one- and two-teacher schools. Small schools have always made up the backbone of our system. Adventist communities, whether from an isolated logging town in the Northwest or a small hamlet in the Deep South, have put their convictions into action and put forth the effort needed to sponsor a church school.

As some communities grew, the small school would grow with it, and more teachers would be brought in to meet the needs of increasing enrollments. For most principals, school board members, and parents, the goal would then be to get the school big enough to provide a teacher for each grade level. Somehow, there was a stigma to being little, or to having a teacher be responsible for more than one or two grades.

Little did we realize, and unfortunately, little do we still realize, the gold mine our system has been sitting on in the form of our small, multigrade schools. Some of the most successful public schools in suburban areas across the country are now intentionally dividing their large student bodies into multiage classrooms. Rather than seeing their size as an advantage, and a way to get a teacher per grade with a self-contained classroom, these schools purposely combine students of different ages into a single classroom because it is good for kids and good for learning. Lead-managers think this way.

I saw a poster on the wall of a K/1 classroom in the Vancouver, Washington, school district. It read:

"It is stillness that must be justified, not movement."

Something tells me that that classroom has a lead-manager teacher. In a traditional classroom the default mode is "You need to sit down, and I'll let you know when you can move around." In a student-centered, lead-managed classroom the default mode is "You can move around, and I'll let you know when you need to sit down or be still." When did we lose the point of the poster? When did we forget that children need to move, and that their learning can be improved through movement? Lead-managers put themselves in the place of their little ones, and they determine to run a classroom that is not designed exclusively for the comfort of the teacher.

Boss-managers work on the students, whereas the lead-managers work on the overall system of things. Also of interest is the fact that lead-managers see themselves as a part of the system. In other words, lead-managers recognize that maybe they themselves are contributing to the problem and are willing to look at changes in their own thinking and behavior. Bosses know what needs to be done and how it needs to be done and see it as their responsibility, even obligation, to make people do it. As parents and teachers we often feel this burden of responsibility.

I worked with an excellent teacher some years back who was a boss-manager. He didn't give a lot of leeway, expected his students' best efforts, tried to be fair in all that he did, but ultimately his students knew that he was in charge. He was the one who called the shots in the classroom, regardless of whether it was an academic or behavioral issue.

It was right about this time that he was introduced to cooperative learning. The approach appealed to him, and he began the journey of incorporating cooperative strategies into his teaching. He had been implementing cooperative learning for about a year when I had a conversation with him that I haven't forgotten.

As we talked about the benefits of a cooperative approach he said, "When I first began in cooperative learning, I would set aside a class period to do something cooperative. I like . . . scheduled cooperation time. As I understood it better, I realized cooperative learning wasn't something I scheduled. Instead, it began to infiltrate everything we did, both inside the classroom and out. The spirit of cooperative learning has a way of doing that. I really began to see a change in my students." There was a pause, but I could tell he was searching for the words. "Mostly, though," he continued, "it has changed me." This teacher was known for his feisty, competitive spirit, so the importance of his words was not lost on me.

His testimony embodies the journey on which lead-managers will find themselves. Teaching isn't something we do *to* students. For the leader, teaching is something that is done *with* students.

"[Teachers] must be in words and character what they wish their students to be" (*Fundamentals of Christian Education,* p. 90).

This theme is emphasized again and again. And as said before, this is the essence of true lead-management. We must decide what we want of our students, and then show them how to do it. What we want doesn't have to be a big thing. Consider the goal of a teacher in a multiethnic high school in the San Francisco Bay area. Every day, before every class period, he stands at the classroom door and greets and shakes hands with each of his students as they come into class. "It's time that I could be using for other things," he says, "but I want to make a personal connection, and I want them to learn how to return a handshake." Something so basic as a handshake, yet for kids from an urban high school, this simple skill can make a big difference in their lives.

There also exists what I call negative lead-management. As teachers we are always making a difference, and sometimes that difference isn't good. Students are being influenced by our beliefs and practices. The same ability a teacher has to ignite a student's enthusiasm for learning can also douse the embers of a student's interest. The following describes negative lead-management, and also describes its results:

"When teachers engage in the work and have no interest in it, the pupils will partake of the same spirit" (*Fundamentals of Christian Education,* p. 254).

Some academy students shared with me their frustration at having to take a regional history class. They explained that even the teacher thought it was a stupid class to be required to take, and that he had come into class on the first day and said as much. Basically he would hand out worksheets each day that the students could answer by studying their textbook. That was the extent of the learning. He didn't want to be there and the students didn't want to be there, so "let's just make the best of it" was the message he gave the kids.

Needless to say, the students didn't get much from that class. It was a memorization class that in the students' minds was just another hassle. In spite of the region's rich past and interesting history, none of that was really focused on because the teacher himself was not interested. He was lead-managing, but it was in the wrong direction. His statements were more blatant than those most teachers are willing to express. He didn't like what he was teaching and didn't mind telling people about it.

Less blatant teachers, though, can exude the same spirit in more subtle yet just as destructive ways. For instance, when a teacher presents a lifeless, textbook-oriented approach day after day, the students pick up that there really isn't much that is important in this topic. Some students, with this lifeless method of instruction, are capable and willing to complete the questions at the end of the chapter. Many more find no fulfillment in such an approach. The results for both approaches, blatant or subtle, are the same. The fire that students have for learning is turned down one more notch. Eventually, some students have this fire extinguished completely.

"Those who desire to control others must first control themselves" (*Education*, p. 292).

The above lead-manager belief is based on the truth of Matthew 7:1-5, where Jesus warns us about focusing on another's faults when we may have even more serious faults to work out in ourselves. I had a teacher come to me after school one day, totally disgusted and angry at one of his student's behavior. He went on about how this student would get angry and disgusted at his classmates and create this cloud of bad feelings in the classroom. He didn't know what he was going to do about it, but he was going to do something. Finally, after venting for a while, he asked me if he could send the kid to my office when he acted up again.

"Well," I said, "you can send him to the office, but I don't know if that is going to do what you want it to do."

"It will get him out of the room for a while, and that sounds good enough to me," he continued to vent.

"But you want more than that, don't you?" I asked. I knew he did, but he needed a little prodding in that direction.

There was a pause as we just looked at each other quietly. His shoulders shrugged and he said, "Yes, I want more than that, but I can't seem to make him do it."

"Does he need someone to make him act a certain way, or does he need someone to show him how to act that way?" It was pretty obvious to me that this teacher was upset at this student for the very habits that he himself struggled with.

The Holy Spirit must have been working, because after another short pause he answered, "The kid needs a model, an example, but I don't think he has the right teacher."

Our eyes met, and I said, "I think he has the perfect teacher. There is nobody better for this kid than you." By the time he left my office his thinking had changed. He still knew the kid needed to change his behavior, but his focus was less on the kid and more on himself. This student would never be forced into such a change. In fact, much of his anger and disgust came from the way his father continually tried to control him at home. Instead of treating this student at school the same way that he was treated at home, the teacher decided to do things differently. The result was outstanding.

A couple of weeks later this teacher asked to visit with me and proceeded to share where he was headed with this same student. "I asked to talk with him after school one day, which surprised him, I think. He wanted to know what he'd done wrong and why I wanted to see him. When the room emptied and we were sitting there, I expressed appreciation for his willingness to stay after school and asked him if we could talk about the "anger" thing. "'I'm trying to do better,' he said defensively.

"'I know you are,' I said, 'and I know it isn't easy' (there was kind of a long silence at this point) 'because I have the same problem.' His eyes got bigger, and he seemed to look at me as if to say, 'Why are you telling me this? You're a teacher, man.' But I explained that I had always had a problem with anger and disgust, but that I was tired of anger controlling my life and I wanted to make a real change. I asked him if we could work on it together. He wondered how he could help me, and I said I wasn't sure, just like I wasn't sure how I could help him either. But we talked about it."

The teacher's eyes were getting a little wet at this point. Mine were, too. He went on, though. "We're on the same team now. We have these little signals when one of us might start feeling disgusted about something. We check in with each other during the day, or after school."

By the end of the school year these two guys, this young man from a difficult background and this teacher giving everything he had to do a good job, became a real support to each other, and in the process became genuine friends. And it all happened because the teacher was willing to look at himself first.

When a student is acting up, it is hard for a teacher to look inward first, rather than letting the kid have it. But before we go on the warpath, it is a good habit to take a quick look at ourselves. Ellen White realized how quickly adults can feel the desire to discipline children, to do so without taking a moment to really analyze what has taken place, and then to think about what is really needed. A worthwhile question for a teacher to get in the habit of mentally asking is *What have I done to contribute to this problem?* or *What could I have done to prevent it?* These questions are worthwhile because they help us to think more clearly and to look for longer-term solutions. They also help prevent what this next statement describes: "When a teacher manifests impatience or fretfulness toward a child, the fault may not be with the child one half as much as with the teacher" (*Fundamentals of Christian Education,* p. 260).

The fact is that many of us have made that mistake. We are tense about something else, maybe something at home, or we are worried or frustrated or insecure for some reason. Sometimes teachers will allow students to misbehave in small ways over time. The misbehaviors are not glaring problems, but they begin to eat at the teacher, and the teacher begins to resent the very behaviors that he or she has allowed. Eventually this teacher will "blow up" and let someone have it. When this happens, the students are confused and hurt, and the teacher usually feels awful.

Alfie Kohn, in his book Beyond Discipline: From Compliance to Community, asks a question that goes to the very heart of what lead-management is all about. Now that you have considered some of the principles of lead-management, read the following statement and reflect on how you would complete it.

"When students are 'off task,' our first response should be to ask,

_____ ?"

Well, what do you think? If you aren't sure, why not turn it around and consider how a boss-manager would complete the statement? Remember, a boss-manager views this kind of situation in traditional terms. Most likely, his or her thinking pattern would go something like this: *These kids are messing up. What do I have to do to them to get them to get with it?* Of course, when that thought pattern is established, a teacher begins to think of ways that he or she can threaten the students with some appropriate punishment, or ways that he or she can remind them of some previously promised incentive. The focus, though, is on What's wrong with them? and How can I change them?

By now, though, you are coming to understand that lead-managers look at this kind of situation much differently than their traditional counterparts. A lead-manager would answer the question, "When students are 'off task,' our first response should be to ask, 'What's the task?'"

And in that answer lies the key to lead-management. Lead-managers are willing to consider that the assignment is a poor one or ill advised for some reason. They are willing to realize that maybe this particular assignment would be boring for just about anyone. They desire to readjust the learning to fit the interests and readiness of their students.

Plato encouraged a similar approach to teaching:

"Do not then train youth to learning
  by force and harshness,
  But direct them to it by what amuses their minds,
  so that you may be better able
  to discover with accuracy
  the peculiar bent of the genius of each."

Remember that we are talking in generalities, since no one is purely a boss-manager, and no one is entirely a lead-manager. But we can certainly choose to be more of one than the other, even if our habits make it a struggle at first. For instance, when it comes to "controlling" student behavior we can choose to focus on what Glasser calls discipline enforcers rather than punishment enforcers. If we are more of a boss-manager, and students misbehave or there is some sort of problem in the classroom, we will focus on punishment and either increase the penalty for misbehavior or increase the supervision, supposedly making it more difficult for students to get into trouble.

Both of these approaches remove any responsibility the student may have to act differently, and both will increase the development of an adversarial relationship between the teacher and the students. The same would be true at home as well. This is not to say that both of these things may not at times be necessary, but a lead-manager does not start with these approaches; and if either of them must be used, it should be done in the correct spirit.

If we are more of a lead-manager and there is a problem with a student, we will first want to rely on discipline enforcers. Such strategies include redesigning the situation and educating for understanding. For instance, when an 18-month-old baby is getting into something he shouldn't, maybe touching and handling a pretty vase on one of the living room tables, we shouldn't spank or hit the baby's hand for touching it. Instead we can use the "out of sight, out of mind" strategy. We simply remove it and store it somewhere else for a while. Eventually we "child-proof" our entire home. Rather than get into constant battles over something children do naturally, such as exploring and searching out their new world, we change the situation or remove the problem.

It doesn't have to be any different with elementary and high school students.

I was principal of an elementary school when the skateboard craze hit. All the kids seemed to have skateboards, and some of them were quite good at skateboarding. There was a no-skateboarding rule at school, but the kids did not understand the rule and did not support it. We were frequently confiscating skateboards. Students were getting angry, and some of the staff were getting just as angry in return. It became an adversarial thing, kind of a competition between the students and the adults.

Some of the students would try to be sneaky and ride their boards when staff were not around. Others would bring their skateboards just to "bug" certain staff members. A number of the staff were ambivalent to the whole issue and thought it was a waste of energy. The others, though, saw it as a rule to be defended. The rule about no skateboarding had been around a long time, and they were not about to lose this battle. During another animated staff meeting discussion about the problems with skateboards, one staff member asked why we just couldn't let them ride their skateboards. Some staff members quickly looked at him as though he had just suggested that we distribute illegal drugs to the students. When they regained their composure, they replied that "it had always been this way," or that "it is dangerous," and anyway, "school insurance wouldn't allow it."

The teacher who asked the question replied, "Well, I don't want the kids to do something dangerous, although they are riding them everywhere else but here. And as far as the insurance thing . . ."

Here he looked at me as though I would be able to clarify insurance questions. I realized that everyone's eyes were on me; they expected me to choose a side, the "good" side of staying with the no-skateboarding course or the "evil" side of accepting skateboards like bicycles or something. I didn't know the answer regarding the insurance, but I liked the question. I said I would check on it, much to the chagrin of some of the staff.

After enforcing the no-skateboarding policy for several years because of insurance concerns, I was quite surprised when I discovered there was no such insurance rule (at least there wasn't when I experienced this story). There were a number of items that the insurance company disallowed coverage on, but skateboards were not one of them.

The teacher who first asked the question about why students couldn't ride skateboards, whether he knew it or not, was thinking like a lead-manager. And even though I hadn't heard about lead-management yet, I was starting to think like one too. Ultimately the entire staff began to look at issues through the eyes of a lead-manager. As for the skateboards, we decided that instead of preventing students from bringing their boards to school we would designate a certain area where they could ride them during the day, provided they were wearing protective gear, such as helmets, wrist guards, and elbow pads.

That decision really had an impact on the school. It opened doors between the staff and students as both sides tried to understand each other better. The staff realized that whenever possible the school needed to accommodate students. The students realized that there were better ways to bring about change than whining and being sneaky. And it was all possible because the staff was willing to look at something from the perspective of the students.

One time after I had presented the Adventist School Journey to Quality workshop a teacher came up to me and showed me notes that he had taken during the day. On one of the pages was a list of questions that he intended would guide him as he worked to make changes in the future. I saved a copy of his questions:

Am I the person I want my students to be?

Are the rules and restrictions in my room reasonable? If I were a student in my room, would I see them as making sense and needed?

Do the students in my room see me as a fellow learner? Or do they see me as someone who does *learning* to them?

If I were them, would I be interested in doing the assignments that I assign?

Am I weaning kids from my control, helping them to be ready to function on their own, or am I robbing them of the chance to really get ready for the future? Do I have some need for them to be dependent on me?

Am I strong enough to be a leader? patient enough? clever enough?

Can I remember the power of example?

He looked at me as I was reading his questions, and I could tell he was wondering whether he was on the right track. *Right track?* I thought to myself. He had captured the essence of lead-management so clearly that as far as I was concerned, he could have presented the workshop.

It is easy to wonder whether we can make a lead-management approach work as a system. Our habits run so deep. Students and parents have different sets of expectations. Lead-management sounds fine in theory, but putting it into practice is quite another thing. Organizations, in general, are resistant to change. The forces for the status quo seem to be stronger than the forces for change.

But whether the problem is lack of strength or lack of patience or just plain lack of cleverness, I think we can do it. I believe we are strong enough, because we have been promised the might and power of heaven to accomplish the task of reaching young people with the message of restoration and redemption. I believe we can be patient enough, because we have the example of Jesus and His promise to "lead us into all truth" and to "go with us always, even unto the end of the world." And I believe we are clever enough, because Adventist teachers are intelligent and well trained and are a committed teaching corps with a love for students.

I am convinced, too, that there are teaching instincts within many Adventist teachers, instincts that are calling them to be more of a leader and less of a boss, instincts they would follow if they felt they had permission to change. Scripture, the Spirit of Prophecy, and current best practice are all giving us that permission.

"Tend the flock of God that is your charge, not by constraint but willingly, not for shameful gain but eagerly, not as domineering over those in your charge *but being examples to the flock*" (1 Peter 5:2, 3, RSV).

CHAPTER 5

To Coerce or Not to Coerce:

Homes, Schools,
Sledgehammers, and Carrots

*"It is, in fact, nothing short of a miracle that the modern methods of
instruction have not yet entirely strangled the holy curiosity of inquiry. . . . It
is a very grave mistake to think that the enjoyment of seeing and searching can
be promoted by means of coercion and a sense of duty."—Albert Einstein.*

During a presentation to a group of teachers, I shared a handout that
highlighted the main ideas of the Adventist Schools on a Journey to
Quality model. One of the principles of the model had to do with coercion, or better said, our need to get rid of coercion. The handout read as
follows:

"An Adventist school on a Journey to Quality will be a place where coercive practices and strategies will be minimized and eventually eliminated.
Coercion, either in the form of punishments and negative reminders, or
positive rewards and incentives, leads to low-quality work and adversarial
relationships. Punishment may stop a behavior for a short while, but it cannot change the heart."

After the in-service a teacher handed me a note that referred to this particular statement. The note began, "This one sounds like you haven't taught
in a classroom for a long time." Her comment reminded me that coercing
students continues to be seen as a necessary classroom strategy and that good
teachers lack the training to do anything different. This chapter will attempt
to define what coercion in the classroom looks like, and explain why noncoercive practices would be better for students and teachers alike.

Coerce ("to compel by force and intimidation"; "to bring about through force"; "to dominate or control, especially by exploiting fear, anxiety, etc.") is not a very nice word. Webster uses such terms as *force, fear, intimidation,* and *domination* to define it. It conjures up images of fascist dictators from other countries, or bullies from a childhood neighborhood. Unfortunately, it can also conjure up images of school. Whenever people must be managed, whether in a work setting or in a school setting, the managers have a choice as to how they will manage. As we learned in the last chapter, boss-managers believe that it is their right, even their duty, to control the behavior of the people they are managing. How boss-managers do this has everything to do with the word *coercion.* Some bosses are friendlier than others, but the basic strategies are consistently the same.

Coercive strategies can be placed on a continuum with harsh, severe practices being way over on one side, and subtle, almost imperceptible practices being way over on the other side. One extreme example of coercion is that of a political or military power attempting to force people to behave in a certain way through killing those who don't obey them or who do not meet specific criteria. The Christian martyrs from the early church understood this kind of thinking firsthand. Fortunately, very few of us have experienced extreme forms of coercion. Still, all of us have experienced coercion. Even in lesser forms, coercive practices damage relationships and hinder productivity.

A continuum of coercive practices might include the following:
>   violence or threats of violence
>   forcing or attempting to make a person behave in a certain way
>   intimidating behavior
>   passive/aggressive behavior by which warmth and communication
>   are withheld
>   anger
>   manipulation
>   withdrawal of privileges
>   flattery
>   bribery
>   rewards

You have probably experienced many of the things on this list. Some of them stick out immediately as destructive, while others you have to think twice about. Glasser believes that the practices and habits on this list make up the reason so many students dislike school and as a result consistently do poor or shoddy work. As a teacher, principal, and superintendent, I saw for myself the high number of students who did not seem to care, or who seemed unable to do the work. Students rarely seem to have a strong desire to learn or to be excited about learning. Glasser believes that if students are to do quality work, and, more important, if they are to grow up to be healthy adults, they must be managed without coercion. Our goal is to understand why Glasser feels that way, and to determine if the Spirit of Prophecy and Scripture can shed light on this position. Before we do, though, we need to meet another writer. In this passage the author is recalling a teacher from his own past.

"What I will always remember about her is her statement that there is no such thing as teaching—only learning. She believed that no teacher could ever teach anyone anything. Her task as a teacher was to create an environment in which the student can learn. Knowledge . . . needs to be pulled into the brain by the student, not pushed into it by the teacher. Knowledge is not to be forced on anyone. The brain has to be receptive, malleable, and most important, hungry for that knowledge" (Monty Roberts).

So who is Monty Roberts? Is he a school principal? a high school teacher? an educational researcher? or maybe a school district consultant? The answer to each of those questions is no. What is his educational claim to fame? He is a recent best-selling author. But his book isn't even about people. It's about horses. In a way, though, his book, *The Man Who Listens to Horses,* is really a journey into understanding people and why we do what we do. It's about our need to control or "break" one another, and it has tremendous insights for teachers.

I first heard about Monty Roberts when I chanced on a television clip that described this man and how he works with horses. The short clip showed how he "started" (he never uses the term *breaks*) horses, not with a whip, or with force of any kind, but with gentle communication. Amazingly, he had a rider on the horse within a half hour, rather than the two or three weeks it would take using traditional coercive methods. I was captivated by such an approach, especially since it seemed to go against the usual stimulus-response view of animal behavior.

I bought the book, and even though I am not a horse fan per se, I found myself drawn into the lessons that the book shared in such simple terms. Maybe it was the book's belief that "what works with horses also works with humans" had me comparing corral strategies and behaviors with classroom strategies and behaviors. Maybe it was the book's describing how Monty feels that he is trying to "change the tide" in the face of such deeply held beliefs to the contrary. He believes that people "can communicate with horses, win their trust, and school them without whips and spurs." Maybe it was the book's describing trainers such as Monty having a "horse-centered worldview" that brought to mind the many times I have talked with parents and teachers about what is meant by a student-centered philosophy.

Monty described how traditional methods to break a horse created "reluctant obedience and resentment" and led to a horse's "working because of fear, not willingness." With regard to one of his mentors working with a racehorse that seemed afraid to burst out of the gate, he wrote, "Farrel proved to me that the cruelty of whipping horses in the stall to make them afraid and want to escape was not only unnecessary, it was counterproductive. It made the horses *slower* off the mark.

"I learned a great deal that day. My way of thinking about horses was enriched by this critical idea: a rider or trainer should never say to a horse, 'You must.' Instead, the horse should be invited to perform because 'I would like you to.' Taking that a step further, to ask a horse to perform is not as clever as causing him to want to perform. Horses naturally want to run, and if they are trained correctly we can harness their willingness to do just that."

Monty Roberts' methods are gaining attention and respect throughout the world. The queen of England is among his clients. There is a growing realization that taking a "horse-centered" approach is safer on horses and humans; it is quicker and produces better, longer-lasting results. Keep in mind that this realization coincides with a growing realization by educators that a similar approach is better in the classroom as well.

Within the scheme of the Quality School beliefs, I think the topic of managing students without coercion is the most easily misunderstood. As adults, our views on how to get kids to behave or perform in certain ways are deeply ingrained from our own upbringing, as well as how we were taught in school. Even our definition of coercion can differ in significant ways. For our discussion, coercion covers a range of behaviors. A basic starting point is to see coercion as forcing or compelling another person to behave in a certain way.

But this coercing can take many forms. On the one hand, we have what feels like negative reinforcement in the form of threats, punishment, and intimidation. On the other hand, we have what feels like positive reinforcement in the form of rewards, prizes, and inducements for good grades or behavior. Both approaches are based on the idea that we can manipulate another person's behavior.

For most teachers and principals this manipulation is not seen as a negative. Rather, there is a belief that such manipulation is necessary if kids are going to get anything done. Instead of thinking about how we can reduce our coercive or manipulative practices, many educators are trying to discover ever more effective ways to get students to do what they want them to do. (One teacher made the comment that "without some forms of coercion schools wouldn't be able to operate.") And so most teachers are on the lookout for foolproof methods to control student behavior. Not surprisingly, there is an entire industry devoted to sharing such foolproof control methods.

Ellen White had something to say on the topic of coercion: "True education is not the forcing of instruction on an unready and unreceptive mind" (*Education,* p. 41).

What did she mean when she wrote this statement more than 100 years ago? The phrase "forcing of instruction" is worthy of contemplation. If true education does not involve this "forcing," what does it involve? And how would we define an "unready and unreceptive mind"? Some teachers would say, "That's easy. I see unreceptive minds every day in my classroom." And while I would agree that far too many students are unreceptive, that really doesn't answer the question. Our challenge as educators is to discover how students become unready and unreceptive. Glasser and Mrs. White believe that a student's desire and readiness to learn are dependent on the source of his or her motivation. In short, do students desire to engage in learning because they see value and relevance and even enjoyment in the task, or because the teacher or parent threatens to ground them if they don't?

When we engage in coercing students, we are attempting to force them to change their behavior. We may want them to stop talking, or to finish their science paper, or to wait in line at the drinking fountain, or to get to class on time, or to be quiet during worship. The list could be endless. There is something we want a student to do, and if he or she doesn't do it, we begin to think about how we can make him or her do it. Glasser refers to it as the "do it or we'll hurt you" approach. Boss-managers with a more positive spirit will think of ways to reward the behavior rather than punish when the behavior isn't done, but both strategies seek to control or manipulate the outcome. Glasser believes that coercing students becomes the usual course of action and points out that "if teachers do not teach in need-satisfying ways, then they almost all resort to coercion to try to make students learn" (*The Quality School,* p. 8).

It is important to understand what Glasser means when he says "need-satisfying ways," because our shift into a coercive response is related to how we teach. He believes that every human being has five basic needs. These needs are survival, love and belonging, power, fun, and freedom. Everyone, from the teacher in the high school down the street to the student in your classroom, always behaves in a way that he or she thinks will satisfy one or more of these needs. Let's take a moment and review them:

survival	These are our most basic needs—such as air, water, food, and shelter. It also refers to our ability to feel secure and safe.
love	Each of us has a need to be loved and to experience a sense of belonging. We have a need to be accepted by significant people in our lives. We also have a need to love and care for others.
power	Each person needs a sense that he or she can influence his or her destiny and achieve success. We need to believe that we can accomplish our goals or the goals that a teacher sets before us. This is referring to power to, not power over.
fun	We each need to experience fun. We thrive on joy and the optimism it brings to whatever task we are doing. Our sense of humor can be an effective defense against discouragement.
freedom	This need has been well documented throughout history. We need to believe that we can make choices.

For a few moments, run your school or your classroom or your home through this "needs filter." Does your classroom provide for the needs that are listed? Does your management plan intentionally include an opportunity for students to have power? How about freedom?

The need for survival is something that most teachers acknowledge but then gloss over to something else. We seem to assume that since our students are showing up for class their survival needs are being met. In this I think we err. I believe that a significant number of our students are wrestling with survival issues, and because of that a great number of them are not ready to engage in learning. Some of them face extremely complicated lives at home, lives that include violence, sexual perversion, alcohol and drug abuse, and poverty.

Shortly after Princess Diana died in a tragic car accident, Newsweek ran an article on helping children cope with grief and loss. The world's collective heart went out to her two young sons in the wake of the death of their mother, who to them was the most important person on earth. The article talked about the tremendous effect that the death of a parent can have on a child, an effect that can literally last a lifetime. The grief can be so deep that a child cannot function, grief that leads to acting out anger, guilt, loss of appetite, and depression.

The article really caught my attention when it went on to say that there is only one thing harder on a child than the death of a parent, and that is divorce. How many of our students come from homes where separation or divorce has taken place? My experience is that usually close to 50 percent of our students come from homes with separation or divorce.

Think now—approximately half of your students are experiencing the worst trauma that a kid can experience. Their very survival is at risk. I bring this up because we cannot assume that our students' survival needs are being met. And because of their profound needs, we need to shift our strategies when it comes to our students' learning abilities. Instead of coming up with more effective ways to make them do what we want, we need to think about how to teach in "need-satisfying ways." Until we begin to meet these needs and to reach students where they are, we will be involved in a coercive struggle.

"We cannot pressure any student to work if he does not believe the work is satisfying" (*Control Theory*, p. 11).

Take a moment to consider the other four needs—love, power, fun, and freedom. Do all of your students feel that they belong? Is there a mutual caring and respect among students for one another? Do students have a sense that they are responsible for their own learning and have the power to affect their future? Do your students look forward to coming to school because it is an enjoyable and fun place to be? Do they equate learning with something they enjoy doing? And do students behave from a sense of freedom? Are they beginning to perceive their own responsibility in what they do?

I bring these things up, not to increase anyone's guilt but rather to begin to show you how far we have to go to change this place we call school. And when it comes to change, as educators we are going to have to approach things differently. Coercion will not work for any length of time, and for those of us involved with spiritual education, the stakes become even higher and the results even more disastrous.

Lead-manager teachers continually focus on student needs as they plan their lessons. Such a focus taps into student interest and energy. Momentum for learning builds as students become a part of the teaching team. The alternative is, as Glasser reminds us, that when teachers don't focus on need-satisfying teaching approaches, they "almost always resort to coercion." He acknowledges that educators can engage in this struggle, but he questions why we would when the results continue to be so marginal.

"We can force students to stay in school. We can even try to force them to do school work, but we will almost never succeed" (*The Quality School,* p. 68).

Think about a time you have felt forced to do something, and then try to remember how well you did on that task, how you felt about the task from that day on, and how you felt toward the person doing the forcing. There are some laws of the human mind, and this next quote from Glasser might be one of them: "When we are coerced, we usually refuse to take ownership of the work we are asked to do" (*ibid.,* p. 96).

I probably shouldn't share the following about myself, but whenever I do share it others seem to relate to it, so maybe I am not alone in this idiosyncrasy: If, when I am driving, a car pulls up close behind me and rides my bumper, I don't speed up to accommodate the hurried person behind me. Instead, I find myself slowing down a bit. There is this thing inside me that doesn't want to be intimidated into speeding up because of this other driver's aggressive preferences. My response seems almost reflexive. Could our students respond to us in a reflexive way when we as teachers get into our "bossing" mode?

Glasser brings out another crucial point about what happens when teachers get into the struggle to make students perform: "The get-tough, coercive approach is the main way in which schools deal with problem students. . . . Teachers who become frustrated by these resistant students tend to request sanctions like detention, suspension, and corporal punishment, but as they use these, they become more boss-like and less effective. . . . This is because as soon as a teacher uses coercion, especially punishment, the teacher and the student become adversaries" (*ibid.,* pp. 27, 28).

Unfortunately, I know what he's talking about when he describes teacher and student becoming adversaries. I can remember coming upon a student who was wasting time in the computer lab. It was obvious that he wasn't doing what he was supposed to do. When I asked him what was going on, he gave what sounded like an evasive answer. Instead of processing the situation in a calm, consistent manner, I viewed this as a power struggle that I was determined to win. As soon as I entered the "force mode" the countenance on the student's face changed. There was a submission on his part, if you will, but he and I were no longer on the same team. Instead of questioning further to determine why he wasn't doing what he was supposed to be doing, I assumed the worst and reacted with disgust and probably anger in my voice.

One teacher came up to me during a break in an in-service I was giving and explained that he knew what I was talking about when it came to that "adversarial wall thing." I listened as he shared his experience: "I came home from work and found my son relaxing in front of the television. I get frustrated when I see him 'vegging' out on television and asked him if he had his homework done yet. He said he'd get it done later, but I answered that wasn't good enough, and told him to watch TV after he had his schoolwork done. He resisted and said he was in the middle of a program.

"When he didn't jump to fulfill my request, I got serious with him. I told him with some passion in my voice to turn off the television right then and to get going on his homework. I threatened to ground him from television and more if he didn't move, and move fast. It was at that moment that I realized the wall had gone up. He turned off the television, but at what price. He went up to his room and shut the door. A sick feeling came over me.

"I had actually thought about my son quite a bit during that day, and had looked forward to seeing him when I got home. And then I had to go ballistic over a television program. When I thought about it, I realized I could have handled that in a thousand other ways, all of them better than the way I had chosen. I could have sat down and watched the show myself and found out about his day in the process. I could have waited until the program was over and then negotiated in a warm, caring manner.

"A few days later I had a talk with my son and asked him to describe his average school day to me. When I heard his schedule, how early he got up and how fast he went during his long day, I realized how anybody with a schedule like that would look forward to a little TV upon arriving at home. My natural reaction had been to go into a coercing mode, but at the moment when I crossed that line, my son didn't view me as his dad and friend. Instead, I was an adversary. Frankly, I had behaved like one."

As teachers we often forget the power in genuine, positive relationships with students. We guard our relationships with superiors and colleagues. Do we put similar energy into our relationships with students? Adversaries waste so much energy and time on the small stuff. Everything can become an issue when adversaries are present. After a short time the adversaries don't even remember what started the whole thing, but unless one of them works back toward reconciliation, the problems just continue to simmer and boil, always ready to take the stage front and center.

Adversaries usually plant their flags over control issues. Teachers who feel they are losing control of the class go into a coercion mode. Students who feel the teacher go into the coercion mode will go into their own reactive control mode. And of course, students benefit additionally from Kipling's Law, which states, "The strength of the wolf is the pack." Remember, one of their basic needs is the need for power. If we don't intentionally plan for that need, or at least accommodate it, or worse, if we intentionally take steps to reduce or remove their power in the classroom, then we should be prepared for an atmosphere of adversarial relationships.

This is extremely significant because very little learning takes place in an environment with this kind of tension and this kind of focus. Glasser sees it rather simply: "Unless we can get rid of coercion, we will not make even a dent in the problems of education" (*ibid.*, p. 70).

The topic of schools implementing a noncoercive approach to student management has been picking up steam recently in educational journals. A noncoercive approach is considered as cutting edge when it comes to educational research and philosophy. Of course, Glasser has been promoting such a strategy for schools for some time. That impresses me about him. He didn't jump on the bandwagon after it had got going—he started it.

Or did he? Ellen White speaks clearly on issues relating to whether we should coerce students, and she did so a long time ago. While I may be impressed with William Glasser, I am awed with Ellen White's views. She wrote at a time when education was in its burgeoning, complicated, formative years. So many voices. So many options. Schools, becoming formalized, were beginning to look like factories inside and out. Students, educators felt, should be moved along the schooling process much as goods were produced along the factory assembly line. And as this factory model settled in, so did educators' views on the needs of children. Children needed to fit into the system, not the other way around.

If a student didn't succeed, it was probably because of his own bad habits or poor choices. Yet in the midst of this adult-centered system, which was high on efficiency and low on effectiveness, there was a voice that truly was an advocate for children. And her views, rather than diminishing, are gaining steam and momentum. Right principles have a way of doing that. Her words are cutting-edge, even as we enter this century. The counsel we have had for a hundred years is clear when it comes to whether we should focus on making students do what we want. "True education is not the forcing of instruction on an unready and unreceptive mind. The mental powers must be awakened, the interest aroused. . . . Then, as inquiry was made, the instruction given impressed mind and heart" (*Education,* p. 41).

It means just what it says. Learning cannot and should not be forced on anyone. Yes, teaching noncoercively would change school as we know it. But the immensity of a task should not keep a thing from being done if it is right. Our focus should be on how to arouse their interest and awaken the powers within our students, rather than on how to make them turn in worksheets. Only as we can connect with the interests of our students can we then engage in instruction.

One of the especially helpful things about Ellen White is the way she gets to the heart of a matter. Her greatest statements cover that which is most important—spirituality, eternal life, and God's plan to restore humanity to His image. Glasser opens our eyes to the possibility of teachers and students being adversaries and schools being less effective, but Ellen White reminds us that this issue goes much deeper, even to eternal issues.

"Those parents and teachers who boast of having complete control of the minds and wills of the children under their care would cease their boastings could they but trace out the future lives of the children who are thus brought into subjection by force or through fear" (*Fundamentals of Christian Education,* p. 17).

If this quote does one thing, I hope it drives home the point that educators and parents need to understand the implications of depending on force to control our young people. If we could see into the future and trace out the behavior of people who were at one time controlled through force or intimidation, we would have nothing to feel good about.

This quote seems ominous to me, and I have struggled to understand it better. There may be more, but I have settled on two main reasons that the above quote is true: (1) it promotes a determined rebellion, and (2) it develops a weakness in mental and moral power. Consider the eloquence and power of the Spirit of Prophecy in explaining these two main points:

"To direct the child's development without hindering it by undue control should be the study of both parent and teacher. Too much management is as bad as too little. . . . While force may secure outward submission, the result with many children is a more determined rebellion of the heart" (*Education,* p. 288).

How simply she describes the balance we must seek—"to direct . . . without hindering . . . by undue control." At this point, some adults are usually thinking, *OK, great. What am I supposed to do? Just let the kids do what they want?* The answer to that kind of thinking is a firm no. Too little management is not good for children either. Yet, as White points out, too much management is as bad as too little. Maybe it has something to do with winning the battle but losing the war. We can force outward submission yet lose the heart. This is one of the main reasons that coercive practices are bad in the long run. Coercion fosters rebellion. People who become rebels, though, at least have some backbone. Not so with the kind of people described here:

"The discipline of a human being who has reached the years of intelligence should differ from the training of a dumb animal. The beast is taught only submission to its master. For the beast, the master is mind, judgment, and will. This method, sometimes employed in the training of children, makes them little more than automatons. Mind, will, conscience, are under the control of another. It is not God's purpose that any mind should be thus dominated. Those who weaken or destroy individuality assume a responsibility that can result only in evil. While under authority, the children may appear like well-drilled soldiers; but when the control ceases, the character will be found to lack strength and steadfastness. Having never learned to govern himself, the youth recognizes no restraint except the requirements of parents or teacher" (*ibid.,* p. 288).

This is a sobering passage. As teachers and parents, we want our students to become strong, independent characters, able to think, act, and do for themselves. Yet, are we doing what we say we want to do? Or are we doing, even unconsciously, the exact opposite of what we want to do?

"The severe training of youth, without properly directing them to think and act for themselves as their own capacity and turn of mind will allow, that by this means they may have growth of thought, feelings of self-respect, and confidence in their own ability to perform, will ever produce a class who are weak in mental and moral power. And when they stand in the world to act for themselves, they will reveal the fact that they are trained, like the animals, and not educated. Their wills, instead of being guided, were forced into subjection by the harsh discipline of parents and teachers" (*Fundamentals of Christian Education,* p. 17).

It's hard, even scary, to think about the risks that seem to come with giving young people choices. Yet, how else will they develop this mental and moral power if they are not allowed to exercise these faculties? I think that's why White encouraged parents and teachers to study how to guide students without forcing them into subjection on the one hand, or doing it all for them on the other.

When you read the following quotations, think on these questions: Do we deal with the students in our classroom in the same way that God deals with students in His classroom? Is our earth, and all of us aboard it, a part of God's classroom? *The Desire of Ages* does refer to our home planet as "the lesson book of the universe." Wow! If what is good for God's classroom is also good for your classroom, consider the following: "Wherever the power of intellect, authority, or force is used, and love is not manifestly present, resistance is aroused in those whom we wish to reach" (Ellen G. White, in *The Watchman,* July 28, 1908).

Even the power of our intellect should not be used to manipulate student behavior. Teachers and principals will always have an advantage because of their position and authority, and their training and experience will also contribute to this advantage, but these elements are not to be used to win power struggles.

"If a man is to be convinced, the truth as it is in Jesus must be presented to his mind, and must appeal to his heart. Christ refuses every other method—everything like compulsion, or restriction, or force. His only weapons are truth and love. 'I, if I be lifted up from the earth,' He says, 'will draw all men unto me.' Fallen humanity is drawn, not forced, into any position" (Ellen G. White, in *Review and Herald,* June 28, 1898).

Should these be our watchwords too? Should teachers and principals refuse anything "like compulsion, restriction, or force"? And how can truth and love promote learning in the classroom?

"The earth was dark through misapprehension of God. That the gloomy shadows might be lightened, that the world might be brought back to God, Satan's deceptive power was to be broken. This could not be done by force. The exercise of force is contrary to the principles of God's government; He desires only the service of love; and love cannot be commanded; it cannot be won by force or authority. Only by love is love awakened" (*The Desire of Ages,* p. 22).

Glasser seems to have been onto something when he recognized that coercing students won't lead to their success. Whether he knew it or not, his insights were based on truths far deeper than he imagined. But that is all right. The Holy Spirit works through many people in many ways. Our challenge is to recognize the need for a noncoercive approach and study to discover how to bring it about in our homes and schools.

While visiting a large junior academy I had the opportunity to witness a student problem, and then not only to see how the teacher handled it but also to ask the teacher questions afterward.

I was present in the seventh-grade classroom at the start of school when a girl entered the room late, obviously upset and grumbling about how much she hated this school. When the teacher, Mrs. Gooding, approached her, the student acted with disgust and anger toward her. "Get away from me," the student said forcefully. By now the whole room was beginning to look at the situation. Mrs. Gooding moved close to the student and appeared to be saying something too quietly for me to hear. Shortly thereafter the student went to her desk, and, although still angry, sat there without causing further disturbance.

At the next break the student and Mrs. Gooding left the room and talked out in the hallway. When they returned, the girl seemed less angry, but I could tell she was still upset. It wasn't until the lunch break, when I was invited to observe the conference between this student and her teacher, that I learned of the details.

When the three of us were seated in a room off of the staff room, I offered, "I'm surprised that you would allow me to be with you as you work this out."

"Not a problem for me at all," expressed Mrs. Gooding. She seemed comfortable and not worried about the future of this conference. "Are you all right with it?" She directed this question to Elizabeth, the seventh grader.

"Yeah, I'm all right with it. I don't care if he's here." Elizabeth seemed slightly angry but much better than when she had started the day.

"Well, let's begin." Mrs. Gooding was going to lead the meeting now, but it didn't seem that she was about to take over. "Elizabeth, when I spoke to you in the hallway at the first break, you were upset because the bus driver had kept you on the bus after arriving at school, and because Mr. Harris [the principal] had called you to his office when he saw you knock down a fourth grader on the front walk."

"It was an accident. I didn't mean to knock that kid down." Elizabeth was still frustrated with her morning.

"Well, accidents happen, but you did seem pretty upset when you came into the room this morning."

Elizabeth had been looking away, but now she looked at her teacher. "Anyone would have been upset after the way I was treated."

"I'm glad you brought that up, Elizabeth, because I'm interested in that, too. How do you want to be treated?" The question kind of surprised me, and it definitely surprised Elizabeth.

Elizabeth briefly looked at Mrs. Gooding after the question had first been asked, but then she looked away when she realized it was intended to be a real question that she was supposed to really answer. A long period of silence followed.

"Elizabeth?" Mrs. Gooding gently reminded Elizabeth that the ball was in her court.

"I don't know!" Elizabeth blurted. "What do you want me to say?"

"I don't mean to make it complicated. I just want to know how you want to be treated." Mrs. Gooding's tone was noticeably calm and friendly. I was impressed.

There was some more silence, but then Elizabeth stated, "I just want people to leave me alone!" She looked at her teacher with a look of *There, how do you like that?*

"And is what you're doing getting you what you want?" This question kind of surprised me, too. Ditto, Elizabeth.

Elizabeth looked at her teacher quizzically and then asked, "What do you mean?"

"Elizabeth, I'm not meaning to ask trick questions. I just want to know if how you are behaving is getting people to leave you alone." Mrs. Gooding continued to talk in a matter-of-fact tone.

There was some more silence, but Mrs. Gooding let the silence pass without interrupting or rescuing. This time Elizabeth kept her gaze toward the table as she replied, "Well, I guess not, since people seem to be paying attention to me." I think she almost chuckled at this insight.

"I agree with you. So I guess I would ask you, what do you have to do to get what you want?"

Elizabeth's eyes returned to her teacher. "Probably stay out of trouble."

"OK," Mrs. Gooding affirmed.

"Probably calm down," Elizabeth continued.

"Yes, that would help." Mrs. Gooding was somehow in a subtly different role. It was fascinating to see this script play out before me.

"I just have a hard time staying calm." Elizabeth was admitting something that probably was not that easy to admit. I realized I had witnessed a significant moment.

"I think I understand, Elizabeth. Sometimes I struggle with that too." Mrs. Gooding looked into Elizabeth's eyes a bit longer, wanting to make sure that Elizabeth had received this personal message. "We always have choices, though, and I want you to recognize that you have the power to do what you want, rather than what other people want."

"Yeah," Elizabeth replied very quietly, "that would be good."

There was a brief silence, and then Mrs. Gooding summoned an even more positive tone. "Look, we don't have a lot of time right now, Elizabeth, to go into this further, but I am wondering if you're going to be all right for the rest of the day."

"Yeah, I'm OK."

"I think it would be good for us to talk more about how people can stay calm in frustrating situations, but we can do that another time. Is that OK with you?"

"Yeah," Elizabeth returned. "That would be OK."

"There is one more thing I would like you to think about, Elizabeth, before we get together again." Mrs. Gooding remained matter-of-fact, with a hint of optimism in her voice.

"What's that?" Elizabeth wondered.

"Well, you were upset because of how people treated you . . ."

"Yeah," Elizabeth acknowledged.

"Do you think anyone might be upset about how you treated them?" The question really did have an impact. I could feel it. Mrs. Gooding let a little time go by, but then interrupted the silence. "That's kind of an important question at times. I think this is one of those times."

"You mean how I treated you?" Elizabeth was recalling her angry words and tone this morning.

"Well, yes, I was part of it." Mrs. Gooding had left it open in a way that implied that others may have been affected too.

"Part of it? What do you mean?" Elizabeth was at a loss.

"Can you think of anyone who might have been affected by the way you came in this morning?" Mrs. Gooding was slowly walking Elizabeth through the process of making things right, of trying to figure out what she could do better.

"No." Elizabeth may have been telling the truth here. I wasn't sure, though.

"Well, I can tell you the whole class was affected by how you came in this morning, especially Randy and Greg."

"Randy and Gregg?" Elizabeth seemed to have no idea what she was talking about.

"Randy and Gregg were in the middle of presenting morning worship, something they have been preparing . . ."

"Yeah . . . I see." Elizabeth's tone was truly contrite, remarkably different from her tone earlier in the morning.

"I just want you to be aware of what you can do to stay in control of yourself, as well as what you can do when you do make a mistake." Mrs.

Gooding remained kind, conveying a confidence in the student with whom she was working.

"What I can do?" She asked this almost fearfully.

"Yes, I'd like you to think about what you could do that might help repair what happened. We don't have a lot of time right now. Break is almost over. But I'd like you to think about it during the afternoon. Is that OK? Does that make sense?"

"Yeah, I guess." Her words did not convey overwhelming support for the idea, but I sensed that she saw the need to do it and that she would do it.

"Do you have any questions for either of us?" Mrs. Gooding turned to me, which surprised me a bit.

"Well . . . I'm impressed with how you both have worked on this. I'm impressed with how you talk to each other." At least I had come up with something on the spur of the moment.

"That's nice. Thank you. Any questions, though?" Mrs. Gooding seemed to know I had questions.

"Well, actually, I do have a couple of questions. For instance, what did you say quietly to Elizabeth this morning when she entered the room so angry?"

Mrs. Gooding seemed eager to explain. "I said it was apparent that she was upset about something, and that I would like to understand what that was, but that right then I was not able to talk with her about it. I said I was confident that we could find a time to visit, but that if she wanted to stay in the room, she was going to have to get to her seat and settle down. Otherwise, she was going to have to wait for me in the teachers' work-room."

"She had created a scene in your classroom, yet you allowed her to stay in the room throughout the day, even when you did not know she would resolve the issue?" I was thinking of how most adults would have handled Elizabeth's behavior.

"I allowed Elizabeth to stay in the room because she was willing to settle down until we could discuss it more fully. If she had not been willing or able to settle down, then she would have had to work somewhere else. As far as me not knowing whether Elizabeth would resolve it, I would disagree. I knew from the start she would handle it."

I turned to Elizabeth. "Didn't you kind of think you were going to be punished? I mean, you did create a scene this morning."

"Well, yeah, at least the old way would have been that way," she began. "In the new way, punishment really isn't a part of it. When I think about it, I really did go into class this morning wanting to be kicked out of class. I was mad. In the old way, the teacher would have got in my face and asked me to leave. In this new way, Mrs. Gooding came up to me and had that little talk, and I knew she was telling the truth and that she wasn't threatening me, so I figured, *Why not just sit down and chill?"*

"So, Mrs. Gooding, where do you see this going from here?"

"Well, it's good that Elizabeth made it through the morning, and it's good that she wants to make it through the afternoon. I've asked her to think about how she may have affected others and what that might mean to her if she has had a bad effect. We just want kids in the room, and a teacher, for that matter"—here she smiled at Elizabeth—"who can talk through their problems and do the Quality School work. I think Elizabeth is in the process of doing that."

On the way home I continued to reflect on what I had seen that day with Mrs. Gooding and Elizabeth. I thought about what might have happened in a traditional, coercive classroom. The teacher would have got hooked into Elizabeth's anger right off the bat, and Elizabeth would have ended up in the office, very probably suspended, with no one really understanding what went wrong. Elizabeth's parents would have been called for a conference that Elizabeth would probably not even attend. Both the school and the parents would be frustrated, because this wasn't really their problem. It was Elizabeth's problem. Worst of all, Elizabeth would have been robbed of a chance to work through what she had done.

This is just one example of how a noncoercive system can work. In this kind of system the focus is on solutions rather than punishment, on cooperation rather than compliance. It is recognized in this kind of system that using negative reinforcements can gain compliance, but at what price? Schools on a journey to quality believe the price is too high.

It is interesting that coercion can take on so many different forms. As teachers and principals and parents, we can attempt to motivate, manipulate, or control our students from different angles. For the most part, we seem to rely on the negative approach, that is, threatening or using some unpleasant consequence, especially when we react in a tense situation. But there are other ways to attempt to control students. And that is through praise, flattery, rewards, and prizes.

Admittedly, it feels better to promise a reward than to dole out a punishment, but at their foundation, the two approaches are on the same side of the coin. Glasser believes that we should try to eliminate coercion or manipulating of any kind. Besides reading Glasser's books, interested teachers should also read Alfie Kohn's book entitled *Punished by Rewards*. This comprehensive book is well researched and will give readers a completely new view of the issues regarding positive coercion in the classroom.

If you are starting to catch on to the principles of noncoercion, then maybe you are already seeing the consistent thread that runs through any behavior that seeks to manipulate, whether it be punishment or reward. If you are still chewing on this idea that maybe coercing kids through positive reinforcement is also ultimately ineffective, then consider the following:

On the one hand:	On the other hand:
FEAR	REWARD
PUNISHMENT	FLATTERY
FORCE	PRIZES

"In our institutions of learning there was to be exerted an influence that would counteract the influence of the world, and give no encouragement to indulgence in appetite, in selfish gratification of the senses, in pride, ambition, love of dress and display, love of praise and flattery, and strife for high rewards and honors as a recompense for good scholarship. All this was to be discouraged in our schools" (*Fundamentals of Christian Education,* p. 286).

The question we must keep in mind as educators is Why do students, if they think it at all, think that a particular learning assignment is important and worthwhile to do? Do they engage in learning because it is relevant and useful to them, or do they engage in learning because of artificial incentives that adults place before them? Do they engage in learning because they see its importance, or because they want the grade that we promise them if they perform up to speed? Without even realizing it, teachers who reward students into performing convey that there really isn't a lot of value in what they ask students to do. There mustn't be if students have to be artificially rewarded to do the assignment.

Consider why teachers and schools are so into stickers, parties for good behavior, prizes, rewards for being the best at something, and in general, artificial recognition. At its heart, we behave this way as adults because we believe students are not capable of excellent performance without inducement. Either they are not able or they are not willing to do what is good for them. But if we can just reward them enough to do what they need to do to get by, well then, so be it. We seem reluctant to think about the kind of learners we are creating year after year, and we seem even more reluctant to consider that maybe the material we are asking students to learn is boring and useless.

"They [the would-be progressives] thought . . . there were good ways and bad ways to coerce children (the bad ones mean, harsh, cruel, the good ones gentle, persuasive, subtle, kindly), and that if they avoided the bad and stuck to the good they would do no harm. This was one of their greatest mistakes" (John Holt, *How Children Fail,* p. 221).

It is interesting to me how enamored Seventh-day Adventist schools are with the "pedestal effect." There seems to be a profound need to create, sort, recognize, and display excellent student achievement. The world does this too. But we seem to be a bit more obsessed with it. It is as though we can be validated only if our students and schools are confirmed as excellent by the world. It has been all too easy to get caught up in this way of thinking; it will be much harder to change direction.

When the focus is on performance, we care more about results than we do about the process. We see examples of this in music and in sports, but the same principles will have sway in English, science, social studies, and life skills, to name a few. When this shift occurs, students become objects or pawns, to be used to achieve an end performance. Music directors are capable of treating students terribly when they, the teachers, have a reputation to uphold, and coaches are not ashamed to have a tough reputation in regard to how they treat their players, how they demand the best, and how they make winners out of them.

Some coaches may have 12 players on their basketball team, with only eight of those players seeing any playing time in games. Instead of their goal being the improvement and enjoyment of each of their players, their goal is simply to win. Remember, it is the end result, not the process, that is important in a "pedestal" school.

Many of us feed into the way schools behave. Parents may be the biggest pushers of pedestals. Try removing a pedestal or even just lowering a pedestal a bit, and you will understand the meaning of words such as pit bull, politically incorrect, hardball, vicious, and covert operations.

Church administration and church periodicals also feed into the pedestal phenomena. There is rarely a church magazine that does not give copy space to a school choir that has won some award, an Adventist student who has achieved a national merit this or that, or the school gymnastic team that performed at halftime for the Chicago Bulls. These awards seem important to us, so it would hold that if we like getting them we would then turn around and give them to our own students. In the midst of our enthusiasm, whether from our own self-pats on the back or others patting us on the back, we might do well to reflect on some earlier advice: "All this was to be discouraged in our schools."

There are excellent things to learn in this world, and there are excellent reasons to learn them, without teachers having to bribe students into learning them. Kids aren't on this earth to make us look good as teachers, conductors, or coaches. Each one of them is a child of the King. Each one is a canvas upon whom God asks us to help paint in a small way. Any practice that tempts us to consider one child as more valuable than another should be prayerfully eliminated.

As we come to the end of this chapter, think about why we as educators seem to so easily rely on coercion as a way to motivate students. We are capable of coercing our students for any one of a number of reasons. Some of the reasons that come to my mind include:

- Our need to control.
- Our belief that students won't do worthwhile things unless we make them do them.
- Our thinking that we look bad when our students don't perform well.
- Our thinking that we look good when our students do perform well.
- Our basic belief that people can be externally motivated.

But just because we are capable of coercing students does not mean that we should do it. One of the alluring things about coercion is that it *does* work. It works, that is, if you are seeking *compliance* from *some* of the students *some* of the time. It works if you don't care that compliance rarely leads to quality. It works, too, if you don't care that compliance doesn't lead to character development. That we can get some of the students, some of the time, in some areas, to comply is not good enough.

A Mormon friend shared the following: "My 10-year-old daughter has been a part of a gymnastics club here in town for several years. This year they participated in various competitions and ended up qualifying for a state regional event. My daughter was very excited about this until she learned that the regional competition was going to be on a Sunday. She came to me somewhat troubled and wondering what to do. She felt that she would be letting the team down if she did not participate, yet it was on our Sabbath.

"Our family believes strongly that our Sabbath day is holy and a day of rest. My daughter knew that, but this was a big deal to her. She was struggling big-time. I could have immediately reacted to her struggle with strong statements, such as "Oh, that is out of the question" or "We just can't allow you to do that," but for some reason I tried to let her know that I understood what a big deal this was to her.

"She went on some more about just how big a deal it was and how it would let her coach and teammates down, but again got back to the burning question, 'So what should I do?' I think it was God who gave me the wisdom to reply with 'What do you think you should do?'

"It would have been easier for her if I had made her do the right thing, you know, just taken the situation out of her hands, but I felt that she was ready for this decision. She walked away quietly, still troubled, but understanding that she needed to figure this out. She came to me a couple of hours later, her eyes a little wet, and explained that she had prayerfully thought about it and decided that she needed to keep the Sabbath day holy.

"Of course, I was so touched by it, and so proud of her working through it the way she did. Her commitment was an inspiration to me. Later as I was thinking about the situation some more, I realized how close I had come to quickly dismissing the idea of her participating on Sabbath. She was the child and I was the parent and this was just something that parents need to decide. I realized that if I had quickly dismissed her struggle and made her do what I believed to be right, I would have robbed her of a significant lesson in her life. It turned out to be an important lesson for us both."

And that is the lesson for us, too.

Rather than coercion, choices;
rather than compliance, guidance.

Chapter 6

Dog Saliva, Pigeons, and Children

"No use to shout at them to pay attention. If the situations, the materials, the problems before the child do not interest him, his attention will slip off to what does interest him, and no amount of exhortation or threats will bring it back."—John Holt.

"You can lead a boy to college, but you cannot make him think."—Elbert Hubbard.

Gwen Webster is standing in the open doorway of her fourth-grade classroom. One moment she is looking out to the playground where most of her students are playing and the next moment she turns to look into the classroom where two students continue to sit. She has kept the two students in because they have not finished their assignment. She had certainly warned them of this possibility, but they wouldn't get to work, so now she has determined to "increase their concern about finishing the work."

Except, as she looks back into the classroom, neither Vaughn nor Laurel seems the least bit concerned about their work. And so Gwen stands in the open doorway, fretting just a bit about the cold of the winter morning air exchanging places with the warmth of the heated classroom through that open door, and fretting just a bit that she can't be visiting with her colleagues, whose classrooms share this recess time, chatting in a small group out by the playground equipment.

As her frustration grows, Gwen Webster begins to think about other ways to make these kids get their work done. Tony got his work done, although as she looks at the disheveled worksheet that he thrust into her hand before zooming out to the field to play football with his classmates she realizes that what he completed barely merits a passing score. Yet he turned something in. *What is with these other two kids?* she thinks to herself. And so she stands in the doorway, her left side feeling the warmth of the classroom, her right the chill of the winter air, and continues to think about what she needs to do to get Vaughn and Laurel to finish their assignment.

She looks at Laurel, who is quietly reading a book at her desk, seemingly oblivious to her teacher's concern. And then she looks at Vaughn, who is quietly yet angrily sitting at his desk. *Well, he can be as angry as he wants,* she again thinks to herself. *As far as I'm concerned, he can sit there until the cows come home, but that assignment will get done.* She looks at her watch. Still 10 minutes to go for recess.

"Train up a child in the way he should go, and when he is old he will not depart from it" (Prov. 22:6, NKJV).

It is the most quoted text in Scripture when it comes to raising and guiding children. Say just the first four words of the text, and most people will be able to finish the rest of it without even thinking. It is a part of our culture. Yet, do we really know what it means? Most believe the text is basically saying, *"Make* a child behave when he is young, and when he is old he will keep on behaving." Is that what the word "train" means? Does it denote "making a child behave" and "control"? People raise their eyebrows at parents who are not controlling their children. And the term *classroom control* is synonymous with good teaching. But can we control other people? And if we can, should we?

∞

The dog sat expectantly. The laboratory environment, which included a white-coated fellow named Ivan Pavlov, created an important feel, although the dog was oblivious to this importance. He was hungry, and hungry dogs aren't aware of much beyond their own hunger. He certainly was not aware of the effect his canine saliva would have on classrooms and workplaces for years to come. Nor was he aware that his saliva would inspire John Watson to become the "father of behaviorism," and he, in turn, would inspire B. F. Skinner to continue experiments on "conditioned" responses using pigeons, although pigeon saliva is much harder to measure.

The animals' behavior, these researchers would say, demonstrated that human behavior could be motivated and controlled through external stimuli. You could, in effect, make someone behave as you wished them to behave.

These beliefs form the granite foundation of our parenting and classroom management strategies. In fact, the belief that one person can make another person behave in a certain way forms the basic motivation and evaluation system for almost all organizations. Managers are responsible for their employees behaving a certain way, and parents are responsible for their children behaving a certain way, and teachers are responsible for their students behaving a certain way, and on and on the cycle goes. I am not saying anything new here. You know what I am talking about.

Pavlov studied dogs and their responses to conditioning. In his best-known experiment, he rang a bell as he fed some dogs several meals. Each time the dogs heard the bell they knew a meal was coming, and they would begin to salivate. Pavlov then rang the bell without bringing the food, but the dogs still salivated. They had been "conditioned" to salivate at the sound of a bell. Pavlov believed that humans react to stimuli in the same way. John Watson believed that people could be studied objectively, with a focus on behavior (hence, behaviorism), rather than on the mind or human consciousness.

Skinner agreed with many of Watson's beliefs, but went beyond Watson's emphasis on reflexes and conditioning and developed the theory of "operant conditioning." Operant conditioning says that we behave the way we do because our behavior has had certain consequences in the past. Therefore, our experience of reinforcement determines our future behavior.

By now, I am sure all of your memories from Psych 101 are flooding back into your consciousness. Probably a picture from a psychology textbook has come to your mind—a picture of Skinner standing next to a table on which rests a Skinner Box with a pigeon inside. He has white hair and black glasses. No, not the pigeon; I am talking about Skinner. Well, maybe your memories aren't as sharp as I thought. That's OK. What you remember from a college psychology course is not as important as what you experience and see around you every day. Suffice it to say that behaviorism, or stimulus-response theory, as it is also known, is alive and well in homes and classrooms across the country.

Teachers believe that they are responsible for their students' responses and therefore they must apply the right stimulus to get that response. Stimuli can be positive in nature, such as rewards and prizes, or it can be negative in nature, such as threats and punishment. By applying pleasure or pain, these teachers seek to control student behavior.

On the one hand, teachers can give stickers for turning in schoolwork that is well done, or provide extra recess to the group that is consistently on task, or provide a party when the marble jar is full, or give verbal praise to the student who is cooperating. On the other hand, teachers can threaten to call parents if students are not behaving, or take free time away, or have students put their head down on their desk, or keep a student from being at a classroom party, or assign an unpleasant chore that needs to be completed. These are just a few examples of what teachers can do. Teachers have an impressive arsenal of stimuli.

Whether teachers realize it or not, whether they remember Psych 101, whether they remember Pavlov, Watson, or Skinner, and whether they can define such terms as *behaviorism* and *operant conditioning,* they are employing stimulus-response theory when they attempt to control student behavior through pleasure or pain. And whether or not they realize it, stimulus-response strategies are based on the belief that rather than having a psyche and a mind, a person has only a brain that responds to external stimuli. Taken further, these beliefs lead to a mind-set wherein we are not responsible for our actions. If we are mere machines, without minds or psyches, reacting to stimuli and operating in our environment to attain certain ends, then anything we do is inevitable. By its very nature behaviorism is manipulative. It seeks not merely to understand human behavior but to predict and control it.

The question is—and it is of incredible importance—Do we really understand what behaviorism is all about? And if as a teacher you are incorporating stimulus-response principles in your classroom, are you doing so intentionally, because you believe in its value, or are you using these strategies almost without thinking? My sense is that teachers don't consciously think about the principles of behaviorism, and therefore don't consider what the long-term effects on students are when those principles are practiced. It is easy to do. The way most classrooms are managed has been in place for so long that we don't give it a second thought. We often feel uncomfortable with some of the practices, even as we might be doing them, but we rarely question the strategy itself.

The world may embrace the principles of stimulus-response, but it is these very principles with which Glasser and White take issue. Glasser believes that it is the idea that one person can control another person that causes most of our relationship problems. (He further believes that dysfunctional relationships are responsible for almost all of the problems, including mental illness, that we human beings experience.) He feels that stimulus-response modes of behavior, or external control, as he now refers to it, need to be eliminated from how people treat one another.

Our belief that we can control another person poisons our relationships and contributes to most of the problems we experience. This is especially true of our most important relationships such as marriage and parenting. Spouses engage in this dance of control in attempts to have their needs met, which are then met with resistance, until a dynamic of competition is formed. One spouse feels a need to change the partner, and the "dance" begins. Parents frequently get into a power struggle with their teenagers. They desire to control what their son or daughter is doing and throw their energy into making certain, at all costs, that things happen or not happen. Often the cost is a disconnected relationship.

External control affects schools, too. In fact, the idea that one person can control another person forms the foundation of school behavioral plans. This, Glasser says, is one of the key problems in education today and one of the keys that must be changed if schools are going to produce quality students. In his book *The Quality School: Managing Students Without Coercion,* Glasser begins to describe the problem.

"Teachers and students are being managed in the same way they always have been, the same way that people have been managed for centuries, by a method based on an ancient, 'common sense' theory of how we function, which is best called external control [stimulus-response]. . . . External control theory is wrong. When it is used to manage people, it leads to a traditional management method that I will call boss-management. Boss-management is ineffective because it relies on coercion and always results in the teachers and the students becoming adversaries" (p. 12).

In the chapter "The Power of Choice" we learned that choice theory is the exact opposite of stimulus-response. Glasser isn't talking about modifying or tweaking the existing system of thought. It isn't fixable, because it is wrong from start to finish: "External control theory is wrong."

The statement challenges us to question the very heart of how we manage people. It challenges us to consider the level of effectiveness that we are now experiencing at home or at the workplace, and to begin to think about an alternative.

Admittedly, when Glasser says that "external control theory is wrong," he is not speaking against the idea of cause and effect. The dogs did salivate when the bell rang. Many students do seem to respond to incentives on the one hand, or punishments on the other hand, especially in the short term. In fact, it is probably because some students *do* seem to be motivated by teachers' bribes and threats that we miss the point. The misunderstanding over stimulus-response lies in the fact that stimulus-response strategies work with just enough kids, just enough of the time, to make teachers think that they are effective. As pointed out earlier, coercion does work.

But this brings us to an incredibly important point. While it is true that people might behave based on a previous experience (stimulus-response; pleasure-pain), it doesn't mean that we can make a person behave in a predictable way. When a person behaves in a certain way, it is because that person sees it in his or her best interest to do so. This is a key point. It may seem like a technical play on words, but the difference is much wider and much more profound than that. For teachers to understand what behaviorism is, and how to move away from an external control approach, they must understand this important difference.

"Boss-managers firmly believe that people can be motivated from the outside: They fail to understand that all of our motivation comes from within ourselves" (*ibid., p.* 59).

"All of our motivation comes from within ourselves." This is the key that must be understood. Our students, as much as we would like to think differently, are not motivated from without. They choose to act in ways that they think are in their best interest. But the key is that those choices truly come from within their own minds. This is the essential difference between choice theory and behaviorism. Glasser says that we control ourselves. Behaviorism says that we are controlled by others or by circumstances. Glasser and others, such as Stephen Covey, say that we are always acting. Behaviorism says that we are reacting. As simple and clear as this may sound, it is easy for educators to get "faked out" on this point.

We left Gwen Webster, the fourth-grade teacher trying to keep tabs on her students on the playground while also keeping tabs on two students she held in from recess, standing in her classroom doorway. Earlier in the morning she had threatened to keep students in from recess if they did not finish their assignment. A number of the students got to work and finished it on time. Was it wrong for Gwen to think that she had made them do their work? They hadn't been doing their work, but she intervened and made them do it. Right? As you are thinking about this, let's examine the experiences and thinking of several of Gwen's students, including Laurel and Vaughn, who are still sitting at their desks.

Avery is one of the students out on the playground. He is an excellent student and actually was enjoying the social studies worksheet. He does well in all of his subjects, even the ones he doesn't particularly like. He likes to read and is good at organizing his thoughts and writing them out afterward. He knows he is considered smart by others and wants to continue to be viewed that way. The approval of his teachers and parents is important to him. When his teacher was threatening his classmates to get to work, Avery was so focused on completing his assignment that he was only vaguely aware of what she was saying. He was now out on the playground, but the fact that he was out there had nothing to do with his teacher threatening him and making him do his work.

Kendra is also out on the playground, even though she is not known for being an excellent student. Kendra is actually quite bright and is, in fact, gifted in the areas of music and art. She isn't that excited about reading, and struggles a bit with writing her thoughts out, unless it is lyrics to a song. She was one of the students that got to work when her teacher threatened to keep people in who didn't finish the assignment. She likes recess and figured the work wasn't that big of a deal. She also didn't want to get on her teacher's bad side. Better to do it now, she figured, than to have to do it at home later. One of her favorite TV shows was on that evening, and there was no sense in jeopardizing that. She didn't consciously process all of these thoughts, but regardless, she ended up choosing to finish her work on time.

Tony was another matter. He is kinesthetically gifted and seems to be a classroom leader, although his leadership is not always appreciated by his teacher. Actually, he is smart in other ways, too, but so far people have caught only occasional glimpses of the kind of quality work he can produce. He is a good reader and writer when he wants to be.

On this particular morning he and some of the other boys had been talking about the football game on TV last night, and that had led to some bragging and such; next thing you know, teams had been divided in preparation for the "big game" during the morning recess. Tony took this pretty seriously and was working on getting ready for the game, assigning positions for the guys on his team and making new plays instead of completing his assignment. When he first heard his teacher threatening to keep students in from recess, he looked at the clock and figured he would have time to get it all done. But as recess time grew closer, his thinking changed from *I still have time to get this done* to *She won't really make us stay in if we don't have it done.*

A conversation Tony overheard between his teacher and Vaughn convinced him that she was serious, though it was too late. Tony panicked as he saw that only kids handing Mrs. Webster a completed assignment could head to the playground. His powers of intelligence kicked in and he scanned the paper to assess what he could do to fix this situation. He quickly realized that while reading the assigned section in the textbook would improve the quality of the answers, one could actually answer the questions without doing the reading. This he quickly proceeded to do.

He presented his assignment, a bit crumpled and a bit hurried, to his teacher while glancing out to the playground to make sure that the teams looked right. "Oh, all right, go ahead," Gwen Webster said, indicating for Tony to head for the door of freedom to the playground. She could see that his answers were hurried, but he did turn something in. His worksheet might have been hurried, but the three pages of football plays stuffed in his pocket were really quite good.

All of Tony's plays were designed on the principle of faking out the other team. Send all of your players to the right, except for a halfback who delays and then goes out to the left. The play is meant to make the defensive team think that the play is heading a certain direction when actually it is going the exact opposite direction. Gwen Webster had just been faked out. As she stood in the doorway telling Tony he could go out to the playground she wasn't satisfied with the quality of his work, but she did feel that she had succeeded in "making him" do it and turn it in. In fact, this was not true. Tony had reasons of his own, motivations that were important to him, that prompted his choice to get his work done.

That brings us to Laurel and Vaughn, still at their desks, and still not having started the assignment. Laurel sits with her knees curled up to her chest (not easy to do on a classroom chair) and reads a book she has brought from home. She is an excellent reader and a good student, even an excellent student at times. She has an inner strength about her that is noticeable, a self-awareness, if you will. Her answers are thoughtful and usually come from a perspective that is unique compared to that of the rest of her classmates. Her classmates are important to her, and she is also aware of and talented with social connections. She has a tendency to be "up" or "down," though, which can be hard to figure out until you get to know her.

On this morning a couple of things are on Laurel's mind. One is not so important, the other is very important. The less important thing is the fact that she left her house this morning without her jacket. She thought she had left it in the car the day before, but when she got to the car it wasn't there, and they were already running late, so she arrived at school without it. The more important thing has to do with the fact that she and Stephanie are in a tiff, and now some of their mutual friends are involved. Laurel thinks, is sure, in fact, that they are going to snub her at recess. *Stephanie is acting as if I should be apologizing to her and is telling our friends that, when in fact it should be Stephanie apologizing to me,* Laurel thought to herself as she sat at her desk, curled up and reading. She didn't want to have anything to do with any of them. *So there!* she added silently, yet emphatically.

Without insightful probing, there isn't much chance that Gwen would know what is going on in Laurel's thinking. And the issue for us at the moment isn't what Gwen could have done or said as much as it is the need for us to realize that Laurel is motivated by thinking and perceptions that are important to her. The teacher's threats did not overrule the fact that she did not have a jacket and didn't really want to go outside, or that she was in a tiff with her friends and would just as soon not have to deal with them right then. Laurel is an example of a person who makes a choice, even in the face of threats or punishment, for reasons that have to do with internal motivation.

Vaughn is another such example. Vaughn sits at his desk, still and seething. His little heart is beating a bit faster, and if he had a pencil in his hand at the moment he would probably break it. Vaughn is actually quite bright, but most people miss his brightness and focus on his "troubled" life. Vaughn is at school because his grandmother is paying for the tuition (she can barely afford it on her fixed income, but the church is helping a bit too). He lives with his mother (another story in itself) and his little sister. No one seems to know anything about the missing dad.

Although young, Vaughn already feels that he has to fight to get his "place in life." He lives by the adage that "it isn't important that you get good attention or bad attention, as long as you get attention." To be sure, most of the attention that Vaughn gets is bad attention. Other students care about what their teachers think of them; Vaughn doesn't seem to. Other students want to go to this school; Vaughn doesn't. He seems to range from defensive to aggressive, and adults seem to talk a lot about what to do with Vaughn.

He doesn't read much, as there are almost no books at home. He doesn't write much either, although he is certainly capable of both. He looked at the social studies worksheet when the teacher handed it out, but nothing on the worksheet grabbed him. It was just one more thing that he was supposed to do in school. He delayed a bit in getting started, since he was somewhat involved with some of the football talk going back and forth. Ted had encouraged him to get his assignment done so that he could be on Ted's team.

Vaughn was actually getting his textbook out of his desk to get started when Mrs. Webster first announced that anyone not finishing the assignment would not go out to recess. The more he thought about what she said, the more it bugged him. *People are always trying to make me do stuff,* he thought to himself. *I don't want to do this stupid worksheet anyway. She can't make me do it. Better yet, maybe they'll kick me out.* At his young age Vaughn had only a vague appreciation for his own reputation, although that sense was growing. Something inside was driving him to be unique, to be himself, to create his niche.

Gwen was beginning to engage in a "fight" with Vaughn, though not on purpose. She would not have described it as a competition, but that is what it was. If pressed, Gwen would have said that "for Vaughn's sake I am going to win this thing." Again, the key at this point isn't reviewing what Gwen was doing. The key is understanding that Vaughn sat there seething and determined for reasons totally inside of himself. Regardless of her arsenal of stimuli, Gwen was not going to make Vaughn do much of anything.

Hopefully you are beginning to see that many students do what they are asked to do, even when there is a coercive element to the request or demand. Motivations vary. Some students want to be thought well of by the teacher, other students don't want to get hassled at home, others want to be considered smart by their classmates, others don't want to deal with detentions or school sanctions, while still others like the material being studied and are energized by the subject matter. These are only a few of the reasons that affect student internal motivation.

Students, like everyone else on this planet, make decisions for reasons that are personally relevant to them. Glasser's friend chose not to give a gun-toting attacker his wallet; the three Hebrew youth shocked the crowd and Nebuchadnezzar by refusing to bow to the statue; usually we pick up ringing telephones, but sometimes we choose not to; most of us, most of the time, choose to stop at red lights, but that isn't always the case. Similarly, students have internal reasons for what they choose.

This principle will change the way you look at students, the way you relate to them, the way you discipline them and grade them. The hierarchical, often adversarial, relationship between teacher and students begins to melt as teachers realize that "I am not responsible for controlling students. They are responsible for controlling themselves." As teachers realize that they cannot make students do anything that they don't want to do, they enter a new way of relating to students, a fresh way of motivating them and working through challenges. Rather than doing things *to* students, teachers begin to genuinely do things *with* students.

"Nothing outside of us, including school, can ever fulfill our needs for us because we can only do this for ourselves" (*Control Theory,* p. 15).

Ultimately, our students' performance is really about their fulfilling their own needs. The same is true about us as adults. And remember, there is freedom in this concept. We are not controlled by others or by circumstances. We are free to make choices. Of course, the flip side of this freedom is that we can't blame others for our misfortune. We are responsible for us. Our students must be responsible for themselves. To understand this point, to believe it and desire its implementation, is a life-changing experience. For me, the changes were personal as well as professional. To see that our motivation comes from within, and that we are responsible for our own decisions, is to begin a journey. To understand that students live under those same principles is to begin a journey with them as well.

∽

The name Ivan Pavlov doesn't bring up thoughts of Ellen White. Nor does the name B. F. Skinner or the term *behaviorism.* Instead, Pavlov and Skinner recall vague memories of Psych 101 lectures and something about dog saliva. We are reminded of something like operant conditioning when we go to a place like Marine World and attend the whale and dolphin show, where we hear from the trainers how they get the giant killer whales to jump high out of the water and touch a large orange ball with the tip of their snout, or how they get dolphins to do amazing flips or to jump high out of the water to receive a fish from the trainer's hand. Other trainers can get dogs to walk on their hind legs or lions to jump through hoops of fire or elephants to balance on one foot.

Eddie, the dog on the popular sitcom *Frasier,* behaved with almost human-like tendencies because of his training. Trainers explain that they reward any behavior, even slight, that resembles the ultimate behavior for which the trainers are aiming. If it works with Eddie the dog, many teachers think, it certainly will work with students. What has continued to escape educators' notice, though, is that Pavlov and Skinner, for all the work they did that eventually created and contributed to the field of human behaviorism, never did work with human subjects.

Earlier I shared how at an evening seminar for parents I had been questioned as to why I was interested in the ideas of secular authors when we had the "red books" to guide us, and how six months later I was reading in one of the "red books" and discovered a passage that sounded so much like Glasser that it caused me to begin a comprehensive study that led to the ideas I am sharing with you in this book. This next passage from Ellen White is the passage that first alerted me to the similarity between her principles on teaching and William Glasser's. It is this passage that I read during that early morning before staff worship.

"The training of children must be conducted on a different principle from that which governs the training of irrational animals. The brute has only to be accustomed to submit to its master; but the child must be taught to control himself. The will must be trained to obey the dictates of reason and conscience. A child may be so disciplined as to have, like the beast, no will of its own, his individuality being lost in that of his teacher. Such training is unwise, and its effect disastrous" (*Fundamentals of Christian Education,* p. 57).

The name Ivan Pavlov might not bring up thoughts of Ellen White, but it should. The name B. F. Skinner or the term *behaviorism* might not either, but they should, too. Glasser says that stimulus-response theory is wrong and that humans behave according to different principles. After reading Ellen White's statement regarding the training of children, which view do you see her supporting?

The core issues revolve around the following question: Are we pawns of other people and victims of circumstance or are we freewill beings with the power to make choices? Beginning in the late 1960s William Glasser began to challenge existing behavioral theory. He did not realize it at the time, but a little woman from New England had been making similar challenges at the turn of the century. Pavlov didn't produce his work with dogs until 1903, and Skinner did his most famous work during the 1940s and 1950s. Yet Ellen White was providing direction in regard to behaviorism before Pavlov's ideas got attention and long before Skinner began his work.

She had significant things to say about the core question—Are we pawns or choosers? Her concerns with a stimulus-response approach were not superficial but ran deep, so deep that she described its eventual result as "disastrous." Sometimes we come to believe an idea because it is the only thing we have experienced. Behaviors become and remain a habit because they are familiar. Some ideas become so ingrained and so pervasive that we view them as unchangeable, too immense to even modify, never mind eradicate. I think the idea of stimulus-response/external control has become immense enough that most people no longer question its validity.

It's a bit remarkable that people, especially educators, don't question a stimulus-response approach, since its implementation has such mixed results. Teachers have known for years that management plans based on reward and punishment are mostly unsuccessful. Some students respond to certain rewards, but over time the reward system causes more problems than it solves, and even erodes interest in the very behaviors being rewarded. Punishment, on the other hand, can stop a behavior with some students, but it doesn't last long either. Rewards and punishment don't lead to the solution that lasts—a change of heart and a change of thinking. There are some short-term victories, but nothing seems to stick. When we review student behaviors over a period of time, we see the same problems coming back, resurrecting themselves in slightly different forms but basically the same as before.

Our challenge as educators is to discover the "different principle" that White is referring to. We must understand the ways of working with students that will have positive, long-lasting effects. We must implement school management strategies that guide students toward learning to control themselves. Such a focus will change how teachers govern their classrooms as they become more farsighted, more patient, and more sharing, and as they work to shift responsibility for student behavior to the students themselves.

Glasser writes from a secular humanist perspective, yet believes that people cannot be happy when controlled by others. He feels that humans need to experience the power and freedom to make choices. Ellen White recognizes this need as well, but she feels that the topic is crucial because of its moral implications. The "different principle" to which she refers is concerned with character development and ultimately eternal life. For instance:

1. Children should not be forced to submit for the sake of revealing who is stronger. People are not to be controlled by others, but are to be free, moral agents, capable of making responsible choices. In like manner, people are not to be controlled by circumstances, either. Most believe that we *react* to events that happen to us, but the truth of the matter is that we always *act*. We make choices. These choices are the result of beliefs, values, and habits. We are always *acting,* not reacting.

2. Rather than simply being good submitters, children must learn to control themselves. This is the challenge of parents and teachers. As fast as children are able, we are to turn responsibility for making choices over to them. Rather than struggling to control them as they get older, we should be weaning them from our control.

3. Young people must be introduced to the fact that they have an internal compass that needs to be connected to Jesus. It is on that spiritual compass that the success of their life will be built. Children can

be forced to submit, made to behave, but at what point does the behavior become part of that child's thinking? At what point does the child say, "This is who I am, and this is how I want to behave"? Chances are that if a child has been forced to behave a certain way, it is unlikely that the forced behavior will ever be a part of his future, adult behavior.

4. The lives of young people without self-control, without that internal compass, will end in disaster. Life is hard. Whether we are well-to-do or just scrape by from month to month, life is difficult. Important decisions are not easy, and even loved ones let us down. We are beset by grief, loss, discouragement, misunderstanding, addictions, competitiveness, envy, and jealousy. To be successful in life, and to be at peace doing it, we must have a strong spiritual sense of who we are and a clear direction of where we want to go. Not where others want us to go, but where we know we must go.

Something needs to be said here about the idea of counterfeit submission, because I believe such a thing exists. In Ephesians 5 and 6 Paul talks about the need for us to submit to one another. He specifically mentions wives submitting to their husbands and slaves submitting to their masters, but I think what he is really saying is that each of us needs to be submissive to others, as Jesus Himself was meek and submissive. Submission like this is not something to be demanded or forced.

It is something that is offered. This kind of submission is offered from an attitude of strength rather than weakness. Parents and teachers who seek to control and who demand submission don't want their young people to be stronger or more independent. Instead, these adults want their charges to remain dependent, submissive, and essentially weak. To me, this is a counterfeit of the real submission that Scripture describes.

Some might also have a concern about the idea of weaning children from our control. Keep in mind that weaning students from our control does not mean that we are weaning them from our influence. Our influence will always be a factor in our children's lives and in our students' lives. In fact, parents and teachers who do not seek to control their children and students as they are growing up will have an even stronger influence in the future. And sadly, the opposite is also true. Parents and teachers who have struggled to keep control of their children eventually lose not only any semblance of control but also any influence as well. The old saying is true: "You gain power by giving it away."

A few years back, when I was a principal, I visited with a father who had some strong feelings about this very topic. We will call the father Roger. I called to set up an appointment to talk with him because of difficulties his son was having in school. The kid was a good kid, but he wanted to be a rebel for some reason. Initially Roger reacted strongly. He didn't even wait for me to finish describing the situation before he began passionately threatening to beat the problems out of this kid. "He's giving us the same ———— at home," he said.

He may have wanted me to affirm his strong reaction, but I didn't say anything for a few moments. I just studied him, trying to understand what his eyes were telling me. Something wasn't adding up. After this silence I said, "I can tell you feel strongly about this, but I don't think your son needs this beaten out of him. I think he just needs you." I wasn't able to go on because I could see his eyes growing wet, and then his head bowed and his shoulders shook. I moved closer to him and put my hand on his shoulder.

When he regained his composure, he proceeded to share why he was having trouble coping. "I know better than to say I'm going to beat it out of my kid," he began. "That is my dad talking through me. I know my son needs me, but I don't know how to be there for him without worrying about controlling him. My dad had all sorts of rules for me and my brother. There were so many 'don'ts' I wouldn't know where to begin. I couldn't wait to get away from home. I hated it there. And when I got out, I did everything my dad didn't want me to do." He paused, and I didn't break the silence. He continued, "Now I think I am creating the same kind of home for my kid. I can't believe it."

Fortunately, that story began to have a happy ending at that moment. Roger realized that what he had wanted as a kid was to be heard, to have his opinions valued, to be able to make decisions for himself. He was able to begin to share the power with his son that he was never able to experience on his own.

Remember the last part of Ellen White's previous quote: "A child may be so disciplined as to have, like the beast, no will of its own, his individuality being lost in that of his teacher. Such training is unwise, and its effect disastrous." Ellen White goes on to describe why such an approach ends in disaster. "In some schools and families, children appear to be well-trained, while under the immediate discipline, but when the system which has held them to set rules is broken up, they seem to be incapable of thinking, acting, or deciding for themselves" (*Fundamentals of Christian Education,* pp. 57, 58).

I used to experience what I now call substitute teacher syndrome.

When I was a classroom teacher, at times I would have to leave for a day or two. Maybe I had a meeting I was required to attend, or a workshop or seminar from which I wanted to learn. I would get things set up for the substitute, and go over with my students what I expected of them, admonishing them to be on their best behavior. But when I got back from the meeting, I would discover a note from the sub describing how terrible the kids were. This would trouble me very much. So the next time I left I would warn the students that for every name the sub put on the board, and for every check by a name, I would double the penalty upon my return. My "get tough" approach totally missed the point.

I did run a tight ship, so to speak, but apparently the tightness was dependent on my presence. Take me out of the picture, and the students seemed to be incapable of behaving as they should. Similar patterns of behavior occur when students leave strict, external-control homes and head to boarding academy, or when they leave external-control homes or academies and head to college. This syndrome should have been a strong indicator to me that a different course was necessary, but I was oblivious to such an option. This is partly why I am writing this book. There may be some of you who are oblivious to other options. Take heart. Other options exist.

Parents can run into this same problem. A dad, like Roger's dad, for instance, can be a strong disciplinarian and literally control every detail of his son's life. He can even force his values and opinions on him, and punish him when he strays from those values, but the dad's conviction will not be a guide for his son when the dad is absent. A mom can manipulate her daughter, and make choices for her that she insists must be made, but her fervor will not change her daughter's heart and inspire her to make the right choice when no one is looking over her shoulder. This is why Mrs. White says that "such training is unwise, and its effect disastrous." Our ability to control our children does not guarantee their future success. In fact, the better we are at controlling, the less likely it will be that our kids will have a strong internal compass of their own.

Most of us as parents and teachers have to admit that we are strongly motivated for our children and students to behave because of how their behavior makes us look. We want bestowed on us the same admiration that famous generals get for leading their troops. We want our children to represent the values that we hold dear. And if we lead a different life in public than we lead behind closed doors at home, then we want our kids to cooperate with that double life. We also want the efficiency that comes from unquestioning obedience and submission. These reasons exist because adults want them, not because kids need them.

Earlier we considered Glasser's statement that all of our motivation comes from within ourselves. Glasser believes that this is how living organisms function and has nothing to do with a Creator, a great controversy, or a Savior. Christians, on the other hand, do believe in a Savior; further, we believe that we are saved, not because of power inside of ourselves, but because of the power of Jesus in us. When as Christians we see secularists referring to power lying within us, our spiritual skepticism kicks into gear.

Some of us would probably say the idea that there is "power in us" sounds more like a humanistic, New Age philosophy than a Christian view of things. Internal sources of power and internal insights frequently spring from Eastern religions and are emphasized by New Age authors. (In fact, at this point in an in-service I was presenting, a teacher nearby muttered, "Sounds New Age to me." Only a few others heard his comment.) It is a key Glasser concept, though, and can't easily be brushed aside just because it doesn't quite fit our spiritual beliefs. Imagine my surprise when I read the following from *Fundamentals of Christian Education:*

"Those who train their pupils to feel that *the power lies in themselves* to become men and women of honor and usefulness will be the most permanently successful. Their work may not appear to the best advantage to careless observers, and their labor may not be valued so highly as that of the instructor who holds absolute control, but the after-life of the pupils will show the results of the better plan of education" (p. 58; italics supplied).

I reread that paragraph more than once. The words "the power lies in themselves" jumped out at me. I read it again. "Those who train their pupils to feel that the power lies in themselves to become men and women of honor and usefulness will be the most permanently successful." How do such words relate to our deeply held spiritual values? How can Ellen White justify this passage when again and again she emphasizes the need for us not to trust in our own strength and ability, but rather to place our trust, and every fiber of our being, at the feet of Jesus? I wrestled with this, maybe as you are doing now, but consider the following:

When Lucifer began his selfish thought processes and began to foment rebellion, could God have destroyed him? Even before angels were influenced by Lucifer's words, could God have been rid of him and prevented the misery that followed? Well, yes, you are probably saying. *The Desire of Ages* tells us that God could have destroyed Lucifer as easily as we can cast a pebble to the earth. But if God had done this, you are probably thinking, the universe would have cause to believe Lucifer's accusations that God was unfair, unforgiving, arbitrary and severe. But then, couldn't God have destroyed Lucifer and also erased from the mind of every creature in the universe that Lucifer had ever existed? Again, the answer is yes. And in that yes lies the bigger answer. In that yes is why there is "power [in us] to become men and women of honor."

God feels so strongly about His created beings having the power to choose that He died to preserve it. That "power in us" is the power to choose to ally ourselves with Deity. God could force us to be obedient, but that is not the kind of loyalty He desires. Instead, He gives us the power to make that choice. "Choose you this day whom you will serve" (Joshua 24:15, RSV). God doesn't want puppets. He wants brothers and sisters to relate to Him within an atmosphere of freedom. As you think about it, it becomes clear that there are no inconsistencies. God has given us this power within, yet as the Scripture says, we are nothing without Him (John 15:5).

This power within is available to all, though. Like the rain, it is available to everyone, whether or not they recognize God as Creator and Savior. We all have this amazing power to choose our thoughts and actions, and to choose the people or things we will value. Incredibly, God has designed us even to have the power to choose to acknowledge or reject Him.

The second sentence in the above quotation is equally as powerful and must not be overlooked. In fact, it is worth dissecting: "Their work may not appear to the best advantage to careless observers . . ."

I heard a story about a newspaper reporter who wanted to get a story on a local teacher who had recently been chosen as the Teacher of the Year for the entire state. The reporter arranged with the teacher to come to the teacher's classroom the following day. The reporter and an accompanying photographer arrived around midmorning and were welcomed by the teacher, who encouraged them to make themselves at home. The students looked at the visitors with interest, but quickly got back to working in their cooperative groups.

The reporter got out his notebook and the photographer got his equipment just right, and then both of them waited for the teacher to start teaching. There was a quiet buzz of talking throughout the room as the groups worked on their assignment. The teacher was moving from group to group and in general was pleased with what the groups were producing. The reporter and photographer sat for some time waiting for the instruction to begin when finally the reporter got the teacher's attention and asked when she was going to start teaching. The reporter had been observing one of the top teachers in the state using one of her most effective teaching strategies and he wasn't able to recognize it.

Careless observation can be the result of a lack of experience. Most of us are content with the familiar and come to see the traditional approach as gospel. A careless observer might expect a teacher to control students through stimulus-response strategies. *Punish it out of them,* we sometimes think. *If it was good enough for us when we were in school, it's good enough for kids today.*

Back to the previous quotation: "And their labor may not be valued so highly as that of the instructor who holds absolute control . . ."

This is really true, isn't it? We do tend to value teachers who maintain this kind of authority. We don't question where this teacher's students are heading in the long run. Because of the high premium placed on this kind of control we are just glad the students are doing what the teacher wants them to do. Yet this is a place where we must act wisely. Absolute control isn't the goal. It isn't God's goal for us. Nor should it be our goal for our students.

"But the afterlife of the pupils will show the results of the better plan of education" (*Fundamentals of Christian Education,* p. 58).

That phrase "the better plan of education" seems important, doesn't it? It admits that there is more than one plan to educate kids. There were different plans during Ellen White's day, and we certainly see evidence of multiple plans today. There are so many new solutions to nagging challenges, so many new ideas and workshops and seminars, so many new curriculum thrusts and benchmark guidelines, yet she reminds us that there is a "better plan." It should be comforting, actually; yet this better plan seems so revolutionary. For one thing, it challenges behaviorism, and stimulus-response, and age-old strategies that we have refined over decades. What will teachers do without prizes, rewards, and incentives? How will we control students without threats and punishments?

Well, hopefully we will embark on a whole new way of working with students. We will learn to place the responsibility for behaving on the student doing the behaving. Kids can be held accountable without bribing them or threatening them. And most important, the "after-life" of students "will show the results" of this "better plan." We are not just discussing what works in classrooms today; we are talking about "forever." We are talking about eternity.

"The better plan of education."

A second-generation Adventist, I have been around the church all of my life. I can remember as a kid hearing about a "blueprint for education," and have a vague memory about its having something to do with Ellen White. Now that I have grown and have been involved with Adventism and the church's educational system as both a teacher and an administrator, I can say that I cannot find the phrase "educational blueprint" in her writings. The closest I have come to it is the phrase "the better plan." She is referring to a specific approach, a specific method, but look what it is centered on—the context in which she is speaking describes an environment based on "power sharing" with students, in which students learn to control themselves rather than simply being compliant.

The book *Education* says that "character building is the most important work ever entrusted to human beings; and never before was its diligent study so important as now" (p. 225). This chapter is really about that study. Character is our ability to make right moral choices. How do we attain this ability to take a stand for the right "though the heavens fall"? How do we acquire the power to make right choices even when no one is looking? How do we develop the instinct to make decisions, not for the applause of human beings but for the applause of heaven? We acquire these abilities as we are given chances to learn to make choices, and to make these choices for the right reasons. We do not develop these abilities as we are manipulated through bribes or threats, or as we are forced or coerced into certain behaviors.

Character is everything. It is the only thing we will take with us into eternity. We will be given new names and new glorified bodies, but those new containers, those brilliant, healthy, perfect bodies, will be filled by the same characters that we have developed over a lifetime on earth. Character is everything. So let's think twice before treating our students like Skinner treated his pigeons.

CHAPTER 7

The Value
of Friendship

A high school vice principal shared his reaction when his principal began to talk about the need for their school to become a school of quality. With quality as the goal, he expected the principal's focus to be on improved test scores, higher standards, increased homework, tighter discipline, and harder graduation requirements. Instead, the principal initially focused on the need for teachers to have positive relationships with students. The vice principal went on to share that at first there was some eye-rolling on the part of some teachers, and there were some jokes in the staff workroom, but in the end all the teachers came to realize that at a school of quality, teachers and students work together in a friendly manner. He concluded by saying, "We came to view the friendship thing as one of our foundation points."

At first glance the "friendship thing" seems to be the simplest of principles, almost too simple to mention. Yet, as simple as it sounds, the principle of friendship is one of the most important components of student success in the classroom. It is so important, in fact, that it must be intentionally developed. It is something teachers and principals of good schools do on purpose.

If you find yourself wondering how friendship could be a foundation point of a quality classroom, think back to that moment you first realized you wanted to be a teacher. Think about when you settled on the fact that you wanted to make a difference, that you wanted to influence society for the better, that you wanted to care for kids, and indeed, that you wanted to be their friend.

You could have chosen any one of a thousand occupations, most of them with better pay than the field of education can offer, yet you chose to be a teacher. Think about your desire to connect with students, to help them realize their potential, to believe in them when others wouldn't, and most important, to show them that your God was worthy of their adoration, and that He wanted to be their God, too.

The principle of friendship was the foundation of your decision to be a teacher. It is still important today. In a world full of uncertainties you made a commitment to be an anchorpoint, to be there for young people who needed someone to show them what "unconditional" meant. When you took your first job, and someone handed you the keys to your first classroom, or first lab, or first gym, or first music room, you weren't thinking about how much money you were going to get. Instead, all you could think about were the kids that would soon fill those desks, or light those Bunsen burners, or shoot basketballs into those hoops suspended above that shiny gym floor. All you could think of were those kids you wanted to reach.

We forget our early motives sometimes, and the raw commitment we had to reach kids. We get busy presenting the content, grading papers, disciplining, sometimes even disciplining in a way that creates adversarial relationships with the very people with whom we are supposed to be friends. Sometimes it is tricky to be a friend, to be the mature one when others seem selfish, to be the consistent one when others are up and down, to be the strong one when others seem to not even care.

When it seems that students are challenging you, it is easy to forget the value of friendship. The simplest things are often the first to go. When sports teams are in a losing streak coaches will say, "We've got to get back to basics. Nothing fancy. Just focus on the basics." You might have forgotten the basics of friendship, but hopefully, as you remember the motives that first called you to be a teacher, the spark within you will begin to reignite.

To Be Liked, or Not to Be Liked

Pretend you are interviewing for a teaching position and you are asked, "Do you want your students to like you?" How would you respond? You might answer "No," and then go on to explain that what you really want is for your students to "get the material." Or you might answer "Yes, but . . ." and then go on to explain that "what I really want is for students to respect me." While there is merit in both of those responses, I would like to suggest that a better answer to the question is simply "Yes." Not "Yes, but"; just "Yes." I make this suggestion because I believe that students learn better from a teacher who likes them and whom they like.

I am not the first to believe that friendship increases learning. White and Glasser, educational reformers from past and present, both emphasized this point long before I came along. I agree with their theory because I have seen their views borne out in practice. Again and again I have seen students who have been labeled slow or uncooperative do well in a class taught by a teacher they liked. And the reverse can be true as well, where a student with a good track record refuses to perform for a teacher with whom he or she is at odds.

I was talking with some high school students about their schooling experience and asked them to reflect on the impact their teachers had on them. One senior girl explained that she had rarely done well in school. She hated school, in fact. She constantly felt out of place, like "a round peg in a square hole." I asked her if she had ever done well in any of her classes. She replied that she had gotten good grades in two of her classes up to that point. Remember, she was a senior, having taken more than 30 classes by then.

When I asked why she had done well in just those two classes and not in any of the rest, she stated matter-of-factly that she "liked the teacher." Her entire high school experience had been affected by the "friendship thing." You are probably tempted to think that she is an exception, one of the extreme examples that really don't represent most kids. My response to that thought is "I hope so." But something tells me that she is less of an exception than we would like to think.

Classrooms as Brain-friendly Places

Our brains are information seekers. They are like aggressive sponges, soaking in everything they can about their surroundings. Information from all of the available senses is processed by the brain at a phenomenal rate. Our sight, hearing, smell, and touch create a rich picture of the events and world around us. Our brain is more than up to the task of receiving those stimuli and processing the information in a way that helps us make decisions.

Our brains also store information. As we process experiences, we come to understand things better, and we gain new skills. We become smarter, more efficient, and more coordinated in our efforts. In this ever-changing environment called life, some things help our brains to learn new skills and store new knowledge, while other things hinder our brains from functioning well.

Only recently are we beginning to understand the term *brain-compatible learning* and the factors that contribute to students remembering information and learning new skills. Susan Kovalik, author of the important book

Integrated Thematic Instruction: The Model, believes there are eight components to a learning situation being brain-compatible. Those eight are:

> absence of threat
> meaningful content
> choices
> adequate time
> enriched environment
> collaboration
> immediate feedback
> mastery

A number of the above components are tied in with the idea of a purposefully friendly environment. The absence of threat suggests that teachers will strive to make the classroom a friendly place. Teachers will model friendly behavior, even when working with a student who is misbehaving, rather than reacting with threats or attempts to intimidate. The focus in a brain-friendly classroom is not on manipulating or "controlling" student behavior. It is on open communication, mutual support, and genuine respect, whether it's between teacher and student or student to student. This type of focus leads to something much different than the usual reward-punishment model. Having students fearful of being punished may seem like a necessary strategy for some teachers, but it isn't conducive to learning.

A brain-friendly classroom will also be a place where students are given the chance to make choices. Rather than a bosslike, autocratic style, which ultimately depends on punishment, teachers will dialogue with their students and together come up with the most effective direction or plan. Collaboration will be commonplace in such a classroom. Students will share in many of the decisions, but they will also share in much of the responsibility. Together these components create an enriched environment in which the brain is free to learn and explore.

Glasser emphasizes this principle of learning as well. A key component in a Glasser "quality school" is that students and teachers will like going to school. School will be a place where teachers are friends with each other, and where students are friends with teachers. Glasser speaks to this "friendly" component when he says that "students will do things [learn grammar, history, math] for a teacher they care for that they would not consider doing for a teacher they did not care for" (*The Quality School,* p. 42).

To Glasser, a brain-compatible atmosphere is a "liking" atmosphere. He describes the importance of teachers being in their students' "quality worlds." Each of us has a picture in our heads about what goes into our quality worlds. Put simply, we place those people or those experiences that feel good into our quality world. Maybe an old saying is the best way to describe this: Students want to know how much we care before they care how much we know. Ultimately, we want students to want to learn for learning's sake, regardless of who is teaching the class. But until that spark for learning grows into a personal fire in each student, teachers can increase their students' desire to learn by being caring and supportive.

Can Liking and Respecting Go Together?

Ellen White also speaks to the need for teachers to connect with students. The last part of the quote should especially be of interest to those teachers who would rather be respected than liked:

"There is danger of both parents and teachers commanding and dictating too much, while they fail to come sufficiently into social relation with their children or scholars. . . . If [teachers] would gather the children close to them, and show that they love them, and would manifest an interest in all their efforts, and even in their sports, sometimes even being a child among children, they would make the children very happy, and would gain their love and win their confidence. And the children would sooner respect and love the authority of their parents and teachers" (*Fundamentals of Christian Education,* pp. 18, 19).

As teachers and parents, we can be pretty good at the commanding and dictating part, but how are we at the "friendship thing" with our students and children? And did you catch that last phrase, "sooner respect"? When the friendship component is present, students will "sooner respect" and even "love the authority of their parents and teachers." Respect is not sacrificed in a "liking" atmosphere. Instead, it is strengthened. And as we have been saying, learning is strengthened too.

One teacher shared that "I really came from the 'respect' school of thought. My early career was marked by that kind of strategy. I came by it honestly. I was raised that way, and in school I was taught that way, so it was kind of the only way I knew. I wasn't real satisfied, though, with doing things that way. When I saw the way Glasser and especially Ellen White explained it . . . it was as though I was ready for what they said. It felt like I was being given permission to do what I had wanted to do for some time."

At the Very Least, Quality Schoolwork Is the Goal

Glasser's goal is to improve the quality of students' work in school. He wants to improve the learning, to raise the achievement. So his making the statement below is not because he is serving on some "touchy, feely, self-esteem committee." He simply wants to identify those elements that will raise the standards in an educational environment. If drinking 50 glasses of cranberry juice a day would improve learning, he would tout that as the way to go. Instead he says the following:

"The better we know someone and the more we like about what we know, the harder we will work for that person" (*The Quality School Teacher,* p. 30).

Glasser understands how crucial the foundation of genuine friendship is to the learning environment. But, you might ask, isn't this just a popularity contest? Shouldn't students put their minds to the learning even if they aren't enamored with the teacher? It is true that very mature people can put differences aside and focus on the work, but how many of us have reached that level? And even with mature workers or students, their work or schoolwork will suffer in an unfriendly environment. Certainly we can't expect elementary and high school age students to look past a teacher's distant, unfriendly attitude and do their best.

Teachers that connect with students are those who show an interest in things that are important to students, listening as students talk about what is important to them. And as teachers become friends with students, students in turn will want to know more about their teachers. This gives adults a chance to share about themselves—significant things that have happened to them; great losses and great triumphs. Students are interested in a teacher's beliefs. They want to understand our values and what makes us think and behave the way we do.

Live an Honest Life

A college student reminisced about a teacher who had arrived at his academy during his junior year. "The guy really didn't grab any of us at first. He wasn't out to win us over or be buddy-buddy with us. And he wasn't particularly cool, if you know what I mean. Sports were a really big thing at our school, and he didn't seem to be into that. He even had the guts to say that competition and all really wasn't very good for us. That went over like a lead balloon. Even though I didn't agree with him, I kind of felt sorry for him.

"What I didn't know then was how strong this guy was. None of us had a clue. It was like he lived his life on a different plane or something. He cared about kids and would do anything for us. He started this weekend service program in which students would get involved helping others.

We did all sorts of stuff. Some people in the church would give him a bad time about doing stuff like that on the Sabbath, but the program just grew bigger. Even the jocks got involved. As I look back, I can see how he connected with kids. He was very real. In matters of principle he was like granite; yet for students, he cared."

As teachers become vulnerable with students, as they share their struggle for strength and understanding, or as they share their beliefs and live their convictions, students are motivated to perform. They become interested in subjects and ideas that their teachers are interested in.

One history teacher friend of mine explained how he got into history this way. "I had no idea I loved history until I walked into Mr. Loveless's eleventh-grade history classroom. The classroom was filled with history stuff. Model planes from several eras hung from the ceiling, while one corner of the room was filled with artifacts from the Civil War. In another corner was this super display on the space program, while not far from that was a booth on the Holocaust. It was like the guy really thought history was important or something. More than all that, though, was how he treated us, as though we were important to him. Whenever we could we seemed to filter to his office. We would stop by to say hello. He had a way of engaging us in conversation.

"I really want to be a teacher like that. I want to create a classroom kids want to come to, in part because of the place that it is, and in part because of who I am. Don't get me wrong," he continued. "I don't mean to say that selfishly, like I am something big or cool or important. It's just that who I am sends a strong message to the kids about who they are. Who I am determines whether or not the kids know they are cared for, that they are unique, and that they are valuable."

My friend understood that his doing well in that history class was to a great extent because of the friendship that developed between him and that teacher. My guess is that if you review your own decision to be a teacher, there will be a similar such person in your background, a teacher who inspired you. Don't underestimate the power of friendship in the learning environment. The brain is a powerful organ, but it can operate at literally supercharged levels when the environment allows it to concentrate on thinking and creating and refining the subject matter we put before it.

Don't Smile Until Christmas

As teachers we have heard that phrase in one form or another since the dawn of our careers. It has been passed on from one generation of teachers to another as sage advice for survival. But as sage as it might be, it isn't brain-compatible. Teachers who use a don't-smile-until-Christmas strategy believe their power lies in intimidating rather than in relationships. In this they are wrong. There may be an appearance of control in such a classroom, but even that appearance may be short-lived. In the midst of this struggle for control, regardless of who wins, the love for learning is lost.

An atmosphere of fear impedes learning. When we fear a person or a situation, our brains click off to the degree that we fear. Rather than seeking information, discovering, and risking, we wonder what is the "minimum" we have to do. In effect, everyone in such a class will go into the "survival" mode. And remember, when the focus is on survival, survival is all we get.

It is clear to me that there are academic benefits to promoting a friendly classroom environment, yet there are still other reasons to intentionally create a "liking" atmosphere. Maybe a teacher described it best when he said, "I believe in all the academic benefits that come from intentionally being friendly, but what really motivates me to create such a classroom is that it is socially responsible."

We Touch the Future

Socially responsible? I was intrigued. When I asked him to enlarge on what he meant he explained this way: "Kids need to learn how to get along with each other, and to value another person. They need an example or model of what liking another person looks like on a consistent, day-to day basis. They need to see that friendship is a choice."

His words struck a chord with me. These kids would someday take their place in society and in the church, and probably as parents. If they were not caring for others while in school, at what point would this ability and desire to care magically take place? As I thought about it, the term *socially responsible* made more and more sense.

Socially responsible. The term must grow on us; it must sink in and permeate our thinking. We have an opportunity to affect the coming generation. We can direct students to consider the responsibility we each have to care for others, to be accepting, and more important, to try to see life through others' eyes. A "liking" classroom will purposefully promote the value of our respecting and liking others. This expectation will be clearly stated and will be consistently held before the students.

Many schools already forbid "put-downs" and kids "slamming" one another or "cutting" each other down to size. But a school of quality must go beyond simply not allowing put-downs; it must actually teach students how to work together, how to be able to produce a better product because of teamwork, how to hear another's perspective, and how to disagree agreeably. The world is crying for people who are mature in their ability to work and care for others. Whether in the hubbub of industry or in the intimacy of marriage, there seems to be fewer and fewer people who understand the principles of friendship. As educators we have a chance to make a difference in one of the most important areas of a person's life.

The Power of Example

The teacher's role in this process is vital. As teachers we model the principles of friendship every moment of every day. Many students do not know what true friendship looks like. They often base their friendships on conditional requirements. They are quick, and even cruel, in their judgments of others. They choose friends based on how another student acts, what movies they think are cool, what bands they listen to, and what clothes they wear. Kids who get good grades usually hang out with other kids who get good grades. The jocks run with the jocks, and the musicians hang out with other musicians. Kids often establish clear boundaries as to who hangs with whom. In some cases students will form cliques that become as tight as inner-city gangs.

People of all ages seem to know that "the strength of the wolf is in the pack." And in the midst of these unspoken yet strong boundaries, a teacher must create an environment in which these boundaries begin to melt. Our challenge is to create a place in which students with different maturities, beliefs, and talents can come together and work even better than if they were alone. The challenge is to create a school in which students see others not as threats or rivals, but as friends.

Creating a safe classroom where students feel that they can be vulnerable, and take off the protective masks they fight so hard to keep on, begins with the teacher. Ellen White recognized the powerful influence for good that teachers can have on young lives: "The young heart is quick to respond to the touch of sympathy" (*Fundamentals of Christian Education,* p. 58).

So many students come from dysfunctional backgrounds. Even young students face pressures and circumstances that most of us have never come close to having to deal with. They regularly deal with environments that include anger, violence, substance abuse, and sexual abuse. Even students who come from more stable backgrounds face a steady barrage of pressure from a world sinking in confusion and materialism. This connection that a Christian teacher can have with a young person, this "touch of sympathy," may be the best thing going for students looking for anchorpoints.

"When I think back about how I was in seventh grade . . . well, I can just say I was a mess. I can't imagine how I must have come across to my teacher and to the other kids in the room. I came from a very dysfunctional background. I never had two parents around at the same time. It was like they were always trying to kill each other.

"Drugs and alcohol always seemed to be around. People whom I didn't know, and that I never wanted to know, always seemed to be around too. I had no knowledge of social graces, no social skills at all, really. I was a survivor. I got into the school because of a Christian aunt.

"The thing I remember was how my teacher treated me. It wasn't that he didn't discipline me. I needed a lot of discipline. It was how he did it. And it was how he stayed friendly through the whole thing. For me, up to that point, discipline and anger went hand in hand. You couldn't have discipline without disgust and anger, and probably rage, even. I would come in with my moods, my attitudes, yet he stayed friendly. To this day, he is my role model. I know it can be done because I saw him do it." That is Maria's story. She is 27 now, with a child of her own, but she looks back to a steady teacher as a landmark, a reference point.

Friendship Is a Choice

Teachers are friendly, not because students are friendly to them, and not because students return their friendship, but because being friendly is the right thing to do. Many students have not experienced a consistent friendship. Most do not know what unconditional friendship looks like or feels like. For them, friendship comes with strings attached. Even many present-day parents act friendly to their children as long as their children are behaving acceptably. A teacher who decides to treat kids like friends may be the only example of such a friend in many students' lives.

A teacher sets the tone in the classroom. Either students come to understand friendship and community and why they are valuable, or they get better at looking out for themselves at the expense of others. Teachers promote this atmosphere of friendship by the expectations they establish in the classroom, by what they say, and most important, by what they live. It is impossible for a teacher or principal to fool anyone in this area, especially kids. To truly understand the meaning of friendship and community, teachers must first foster a spirit of forgiveness and acceptance in themselves. They must consciously guard against a spirit of criticism and judgment. They must remember that each student is of inestimable value.

Spiritually Accurate

A hand went up during a discussion on this "friendship thing," and a teacher from a two-teacher school said, "I agree that this kind of friendship emphasis is socially responsible, but more important to me is the fact that it is spiritually accurate." Spiritually accurate. As that simple phrase echoed in my thinking, I remembered the great Christian principles that guide and motivate us. I realized what a tremendous advantage our schools should have in this area, considering that the Holy Spirit will endorse and bless our efforts. As you reflect on how a "liking" classroom relates to spiritual principles, consider the following passage from Ellen White: "You must win their affection, if you would impress religious truth upon their heart" (*Fundamentals of Christian Education,* p. 68).

I am struck by two points in the above quote. The first point is her use of the word "win." What does it mean to win their affection? It doesn't sound like a passive process, something to enjoy *if* it happens. The word "win" suggests an active pursuit of a positive relationship. It suggests effort and strategy. It means not giving up when the going gets tough. The second point is her emphasizing that friendship is a key if we are to "impress religious truth" upon their hearts. Isn't that the business we are all in? Isn't impressing religious truth upon our students' hearts our deep desire? It doesn't matter what we teach—shop, keyboarding, choir, or English—making lifelong, positive, religious impressions on our students is why we do what we do. The connection between our friendship with students and our ability to impart spiritual truths is so important.

The following passage from *Counsels to Parents, Teachers, and Students* also speaks of the importance of friendship, and it does so from the perspective of Christian fellowship between teacher and student: "Teachers and students are to come close together in Christian fellowship. The youth will make many mistakes, and the teacher is never to forget to be compassionate and courteous. Never is he to seek to show his superiority. . . . Let teachers remember their own faults and mistakes, and strive earnestly to be what they wish their students to become. . . . Make friends of them. Give them practical evidence of your unselfish interest in them" (p. 269).

"Make friends of them." The statement couldn't be clearer. Four simple words, yet our success as teachers, and our students' success, may hinge on them. Four simple words. Maybe we should place those words in a strategic location where we will be reminded every now and then. Maybe write the letters M F O T on a 3" x 5" card and tape it to our desk. Somehow we need to remember this crucial point.

The teacher who shared the phrase "spiritually accurate" got me to thinking of all the places where the Bible speaks to the need for community, togetherness, and compassion for others. More than half of the Ten Commandments address our relationship with others. The prophets of the Old Testament consistently reminded God's people to care for the homeless, the widows, the orphans, the strangers in the land, the imprisoned, and the hurting. "He has shown you . . . , O man, what is good, but to do justly, to love mercy, and to walk humbly with your God" (Micah 6:8, NKJV).

In the best sermon ever, Jesus inspired people to love their enemies. If He had been talking to a group of teachers, maybe Matthew 5:43-48 would have gone something like this: "And remember, good teachers like their students even when they are unlikable. Oh, sure, a lot of teachers like their students when the students like them back, but I say show your 'liking' spirit to those students who seem to deserve it least." A teacher may be the only person who will ever show kids how people can like each other even when they disagree with each other.

Genuine Versus Familiar

A teacher came up to me after a talk I gave that included comments on the need for friendship between teacher and students. She agreed with what I had said, but felt that one of the teachers from her school would take my comments in the wrong way. She felt certain that this teacher would feel affirmed in his "buddy-buddy" style with the kids, a style that frequently seemed inappropriate. She described his disregard, when he supervised, for rules that the staff had agreed upon. He exchanged off-color jokes with students between classes, or would come up behind one of them and grab them in a headlock. Students confided to other staff that this teacher bothered them.

This teacher's problem was that he had gone from being genuine to being familiar. Familiarity is a counterfeit for genuine friendship, and, as the old saying goes, familiarity breeds contempt. Kids, even young students, seem to be able to tell when an adult is being genuine. They can see through a fake. Some folk might remind us that even Ellen White said that we should become like a child among children. I would agree that is often true, but there is a difference between being childlike and being childish.

A teacher can attempt to "buy" students' friendship by being a buddy to them, by slipping into childish behavior to impress them that he or she is one of them. But this always backfires, usually sooner rather than later. The teacher, instead of getting closer to the students, loses the chance to make a lasting difference in their lives. When we are more concerned about what students think about us than we are about doing the right thing, then we have entered the "familiar" zone.

Few Gifts So Valuable

Some seem to think that if we focus on creating a "liking" classroom, a classroom in which students and teachers are friends, it will be a place in which students will be permitted to do anything that they want. It is important to understand that this is not the case. A "liking" classroom can have routines and rules, and those rules can and should be enforced. In fact, the standard for behavior in a "liking" classroom will be higher than standards I frequently see in traditional classrooms.

Rather than students doing what they want at others' expense, students in a classroom in which genuine friendship is the norm will behave with their classmates' feelings in mind. When a problem occurs, they will feel a responsibility to fix it. Instead of causing a hurt and "doing the time" (missing recess, writing sentences, staying after school), students will want to restore the trust on which the classroom management is based.

For me, one of Ellen White's quotes brings together in a simple yet elegant manner everything that this chapter really wants to say: "The true teacher can impart to his pupils few things so valuable as the gift of his own companionship" (*Education*, p. 212).

Whether it helps create a more brain-compatible learning atmosphere, or because it is socially responsible, or, most important, because it is spiritually accurate, this "friendship thing" is a big deal. It is vital for a student's readiness to learn. It is part of what gets students ready to learn, and keeps them interested in learning. And it underlines the importance of the teacher, not just what he or she does, but who he or she is.

Teachers make such a profound difference in the lives of the students they touch. A teacher's beliefs and values resonate through his or her words and deeds—sometimes in loud fanfare, echoing around the campus in obvious tones; sometimes in quiet, single notes, almost invisible, so quiet you wonder what you saw, but you know it is there. A firmness, a foundation, a deep belief that friendship and community are important. As a great education reformer once said: "There are few things so valuable."

"The nature of relationships among the adults who inhabit a school has more to do with the school's quality and character, and the accomplishments of its pupils, than any other factor" (Roland Barth).

CHAPTER 8

Getting Into and Out of Trouble

"I was horrified to find my son eating out of the sugar bowl.
'Don't let me catch you doing that again,' I scolded. My boy was willing,
but dubious. 'I'll try, Mommy,' he told me,
'but you walk so quiet sometimes.'"—Pat Bevans.

A s the fourth-grade teacher described the incident to me, I was surprised that the ninth grader involved was Trevor. She explained that her students had reported that Trevor had cornered them in the hallway and threatened them and used bad language in the process. I told her that I would look into it. Upper-grade students bullying lower-grade students through intimidation, threats, and inappropriate language was not the kind of school atmosphere for which we were striving.

School was close to being out when this was reported to me, so I decided to wait until after school to work on it. When the final bell rang, I was waiting in the hallway as the students headed to the buses.

The hallway was congested with the usual after-school traffic, but as Trevor passed by me I asked him if I could talk with him for a moment. We were next to the library door and I opened it for us to step into the dim and quiet room. The library had closed earlier in the afternoon, and now it was a peaceful oasis amid the after-school rush. Trevor looked at me, wondering what I might want.

"It's come to my attention, Trevor, that you may have had a confrontation with some fourth graders, and that you used inappropriate language in the process." Before I finished speaking, Trevor's head dropped down, and instead of looking at me he was looking at the floor. Except for the sounds from the hallway, the room remained quiet. I didn't say anything more at that point. I knew that Trevor had heard me and that the ball was in his court.

I have come to learn that being comfortable with silence is important when working with students as they are getting out of trouble. Some educators unwittingly rob students of taking responsibility for their actions by feeling they must fill the silence whenever it lasts more than a few seconds. They feel that students need help, and they rush in way too soon. Many students are aware of these helpful tendencies on the part of adults and simply sit back, stay quiet, and let the adult figure out the solution.

"It's not me." His head was still down, and he did not say it very loud, more a mumble than a clear statement. I thought I had heard what he said, yet I wasn't totally sure. I asked him to say it one more time. His eyes came up a bit, and he repeated, "It's not me." His eyes connected with mine for just a moment.

"You mean 'it's not me' in that you didn't do it or that—"

I couldn't finish my question. "No, I did it . . . But it isn't me." Our eyes met a little longer. "That's not the kind of person I am."

"I realize that," I concurred. "I was surprised to hear of the possibility that you were involved."

This was an important moment for me. Like most principals, I had always struggled to be fair and consistent and wise when it came to discipline and punishment. Now I was convinced that there was a better way to go than simply punishing students. Not many months before, I had struggled with what to do with a student who had used the d word during physical education class. He had swept the parking lot for a couple days—reflective labor, as we affectionately referred to it. A bit later, when a student had used the f word, my brain tried to evaluate and process and mete out a remarkably wise and fair corrective measure. As I stood there looking at Trevor, his head down again, somehow my meting out anything seemed less than effective.

"Trevor," I began, "it seems to me that you made a mistake in the way you treated these fourth-grade students. I could probably do the principal thing and try to figure out a punishment for you, but I am frustrated with that, because, for one thing, it doesn't seem to work that well." Trevor was looking at me now. He was wondering where I was headed with this kind of talk. "It seems to me," I continued, "that there is really only one question worth asking at this point, and that question is What are you going to do to fix this?" Silence again. Trevor was waiting for me to do the adult thing and keep going on the roll I was on. I didn't say anything, though; I just kept looking at him, waiting for him to answer the question.

When he realized that I wasn't going to say any more at that point and that I was actually expecting him to answer the question, he began talking, but not in answer to the question. Instead, he described to me what had taken place with the boys, how there was another side to the story, and how one of the boys was especially annoying. I knew the boy he was referring to and that the boy could be a difficult person indeed. I interrupted him and gently asked, "Trevor, did you do what I described earlier?"

"Yes." Trevor seemed to know where this was going.

"Then we are back to just one question. What are going to do to fix this?"

There was silence again, but I could tell that Trevor was thinking. Even his body language was changing. He was standing a bit straighter. "Well, I guess I should apologize to Grant." Grant was the challenging fourth grader who had received the brunt of Trevor's verbal anger.

"Yes, I agree. Making it right is important. It doesn't feel good to have anger and bad language directed at you. Anything else?"

"Well, I should probably make it right with the other students that were there." He was looking at me consistently now.

"That sounds good. I'm sure they were affected too. Anything else?" I was more in a coach role, someone helping him think through this.

"No, I think that covers it." Those were the people present, and he was thinking that if he made things right with them, he was pretty much done.

"How about Mrs. Dannon?" I asked. "If you were the fourth-grade teacher and you heard that a ninth-grader had threatened your students, how would you feel about that?" I said this matter-of-factly. He knew that I was not accusing him, but instead just helping him to think through the situation.

"I guess I need to talk with her, too."

"Do you need my help with any of this?" My role was significantly different than a few months before, when I was struggling with how to punish fairly.

"No, I can do it." Trevor had changed dramatically during our short time together in the library. He had gone from an embarrassed, guilty ninth-grader to a humble yet hopeful young man.

"You understand that I will need to check on how your efforts go? I will give you some time, but then I will want to talk with Mrs. Dannon and with Grant, as well as the other boys who were present."

"I understand. That's OK with me." I would often follow up in this way. I felt that accountability was important. In most cases students made things right with people in a very acceptable manner, but occasionally the student would not do it very well, or would skip it altogether. When that happened, I wanted to be able to work with that student in a way that helped him or her grow. Punishment is not the goal—changing hearts is the goal.

In Trevor's case he followed up with Mrs. Dannon and with the boys just as he said he would. I don't think what he did was easy, especially with Grant, who had probably goaded Trevor to some extent, but making things right rarely is easy; it is often hard. Trevor would have preferred being punished and doing some reflective labor, but what an opportunity would have been lost.

Not only was Trevor's heart affected through this process, other advantages became apparent to me as well. For instance, he modeled Christian behavior to the lower-grade students when he talked to them and asked their forgiveness; Mrs. Dannon became even more interested in a process that had this kind of effect on a teenager; and my relationship with Trevor was strengthened as well.

Trevor's story is important to me for several reasons. It was my first attempt at redemptive management and marked a new beginning for me as a school principal and teacher. It also became part of a remarkable new friendship, a friendship that has come to mean a lot to me.

Beginning of a Friendship

In the summer of 2000 the Seventh-day Adventist Church did something that had never been done before. In August of that year the North American Division called together all of the Seventh-day Adventist educators throughout the United States and Canada. It was an unprecedented event, with more than 6,000 teachers and administrators heeding the call and traveling to Dallas, Texas, for four days of in-service and fellowship. Convention attendees benefited from a rich array of breakout sessions, along with inspiration and challenge from impressive keynote speakers, one of whom was William Glasser. I was fortunate to be able to attend the Dallas convention, notwithstanding the August heat, and even presented several of the breakout sessions. One such session was on the Glasser/White correlation.

I had brought along several boxes of materials to hand out during my presentations. Upon arriving in Dallas, I had stored them in the Adams Mark Hotel, where the convention was to take place. The evening before one of my presentations I went to the storage room and presented my claim tickets to pick up some of the materials, in preparation for the following day. As I stood in the lobby waiting for my boxes I looked around and took in the busyness, the coming and going, the many faces I recognized from 22 years of working in the Adventist education system.

Then my eyes fell on a face that gave me a little start. Fifteen feet away stood William Glasser. He too was looking around. *Wow,* I thought to myself, *William Glasser, right there.* I looked to the storage-area counter and saw that my boxes had still not materialized, and then back to Glasser. Here was the man, just a few feet away, who had meant so much to me in my efforts to understand the kind of place that schools should be, and who had such an influence on my personal thinking. I decided to say hello, so I walked over to him and said, "Dr. Glasser, I want you to know how glad we are that you are here."

"Well, I might not be staying," he replied.

The speed of his reply, combined with the directness of his statement, took me by surprise, and I think I might have stood there with a look on my face that said *Excuse me?* although no words came out of my mouth.

"They don't have a room for us," he added, and with this he looked past me to the far side of the lobby toward the check-in counter. The situation was now quickly becoming clear to me. One of the convention's keynote speakers was standing in the lobby, with his wife standing near the check-in counter, wondering what to do next in the midst of confusion over his lodging arrangements.

We walked over to the counter, where I met his wife, Carleen. I assured them both that this was a simple mistake of some sort that would be quickly fixed; I also offered apologies for any frustration this was causing them. I moved to the counter, where I talked to a check-in person myself, naively thinking that I could clear this thing up. It soon became apparent that someone with more clout than I had would be needed to fix the situation.

So now three of us were frustrated. The three of us, the Glassers and I, huddled once again and developed a plan that sounded good to all of us. They would head to the restaurant there in the hotel while I would look for someone that could assist in getting them a room. Thus began an interesting evening. First, to the storage counter to ask them to hold the boxes for a while longer, then to different parts of the huge hotel, looking for a person of influence. Then phone calls, resulting in the discovery that most of the influential people had gone to a Texas Rangers baseball game in Arlington; more phone calls.

After I had found someone who could fix the problem, I made my way back to the restaurant and updated the Glassers. By now they were chuckling about there being "no room in the inn." They were gracious and expressed confidence that the situation would be corrected. While they waited for their food we chatted.

The thought occurred to me as I stood there that here I was with William Glasser . . . and I did have a few questions that I would really like to ask him . . . and what was the chance that I would ever have such an opportunity again? So I fumbled around, probably hemming and hawing, and finally got out something along the lines that "I have some questions I would like to ask you."

Their food had just arrived, but he replied, "Look, if you'll promise to pick me up in the morning and take me to wherever it is I am speaking, I'll tell you whatever you want to know." I was getting my first glimpse at his dry, wonderful sense of humor.

"That sounds like a deal to me," I responded.

"Good," he continued. "Pull up a chair, and we'll visit."

For more than an hour the three of us visited on topics related to choice theory and the quality school. Mrs. Glasser herself is an accomplished author and senior instructor in choice theory, and her experience and insight added much to the dinner conversation, as it has continued to do so since.

One thing I wanted to understand was why Glasser had distanced himself from a concept called restitution. He actually had done more than distance himself; he had voiced rather strong opinions against its use. He had written these opinions in *Choice Theory: A New Psychology of Personal Freedom* (1998) and in memorandums to his senior trainers. He indicated to them that they should no longer advocate the use of restitution.

His explanation reflected his strong belief that one person should not control or attempt to control another person. External control in its many forms is the cause of dysfunctional relationships and poor-quality work. He felt that restitution frequently was being used in an effort to make students behave in a certain way, and that its affiliation with choice theory was causing harmful and unnecessary confusion.

I asked him if I could share a discipline scenario that I had worked through as a principal, with the idea that he would tell me where I had messed up or deviated from a choice theory approach. I then shared

Trevor's story. After finishing the tale of Trevor and how I asked him how he was going to fix the problem with the fourth graders, I waited for the analysis to begin.

I was a little surprised when Glasser responded, "I really don't have a problem with how you handled it." The issue lies in the locus of control. Is the person, in this case a student, operating from a sense of self-control, or is he or she operating from an element of "other" control? It is "other" control that Glasser wants to eliminate.

The following day I did pick him up, and we went to the main hall, where he presented to 4,500 Adventist educators the ideas of choice theory and effective educational strategies. Afterward he and Carleen presented a breakout session that more than 600 people attended. I was presenting one of my breakouts at the same time, so was not able to attend, but a number of others who did shared with me that he had spoken about our conversation the evening before and that he and Carleen had role-played Trevor's story in front of the whole group.

Some special things came out of that convention experience. One thing special for me was that Glasser asked me to review what, at the time, was his latest manuscript and to consider writing a statement for the jacket cover of the book. *Every Student Can Succeed* was published shortly thereafter, and, sure enough, my testimonial appeared on the cover.

A much more important thing that came out of the convention was Glasser's deep interest in the Seventh-day Adventist educational system. Since Dallas he has given several presentations and in-services to Adventist principals and teachers and has expressed how impressed he is with our system of schools. The Northern California Conference, in cooperation with Pacific Union College, had Glasser present a full day on the topic Every Student Can Succeed. The response was very positive.

David Escobar, superintendent of education for the Northern California Conference, began dialoging with Glasser about further training for the schools and teachers who really wanted to understand and implement what he was describing. Glasser and his trainers worked out a plan that accommodated more than 150 Adventist educators, taking them through the basic week and the advanced week training. Senior trainers from around the United States and Canada come to the Pacific Union College campus several times a year and share choice theory with Adventist educators.

This has been a two-way relationship, though. Adventists have benefited from Glasser's ideas and the trainers who share those ideas, but he and his trainers have benefited as well. Glasser and a number of his trainers have heard presentations on the content of this book, and have expressed interest in the ideas of Ellen White. After reading those ideas, one trainer expressed that "Ellen White was really the original choice theorist." Some wonderful Christian men and women have come as trainers and have been touched by the talent and spirit of the Adventist teachers they were teaching. They, like Glasser before them, are impressed with Adventist education.

And so Trevor's story was a part of something special. For me personally, it was part of the beginning of a friendship with Bill and Carleen Glasser. On a larger scale, though, it was part of a growing relationship between Glasser's Quality School Institute and Adventist education. It is interesting to consider how one institution might affect the other in the future, and inspiring to think about what the result could be.

Now let's get back to the point of this chapter, a study of the topic of discipline and management. Key questions include How do you keep students from getting into trouble? and If they get into trouble, how do you respond? To answer these questions we will continue to consider the ideas and counsel of William Glasser and Ellen White. In the process I will introduce redemptive management, which incorporates the effective parts of restitution while leaving off the elements of external control.

An Ounce of Prevention Is Worth a Pound of Cure

Classrooms that run smoothly and effectively are the desire and goal of every educator I know. To have a classroom in which students learn and in which people treat each other well is like a dream come true. Teaching becomes extremely satisfying when classroom management is working well. Teachers go home after school and arrive at work the next morning with more energy and optimism when management is not an issue.

Unfortunately, the opposite is true too. Teaching becomes a drudgery or worse when classroom management isn't working well. An uncomfortable atmosphere exists in such a classroom, and soon most people, including the teacher, don't want to be in that room. When teachers have to start over at another school or leave the teaching profession entirely, it is often because of bad experiences with management.

When classroom management begins to go bad, teachers often view the solution in terms of a need to get tougher. Threats and punishments are the usual result. Teachers also throw in some intimidation for good measure. Most see classroom control as a product of the behaviors they reward or punish. Students will come into line as rules are enforced and punishments are meted out. I have observed such an approach implemented in classrooms, and the results aren't pretty. Glasser helps us understand why:

"We are much too concerned with discipline, with how to "make" students follow rules, and not enough concerned with providing the satisfying education that would make our concern with discipline unnecessary. To focus on discipline is to ignore the real problem" (*Control Theory,* p. 12).

One of the keys to effective classroom management is to recognize its connection with instruction. When ineffective management is analized, this is almost always overlooked. Glasser emphasizes three basic components that need to be present in classrooms.

1. Supportive, nurturing environment.
2. Relevant, useful schoolwork.
3. Self-assessment.

His belief is that when students are in a classroom in which their teacher cares about them and classmates care about one another, and in which the work they are asked to do is meaningful and interesting, there will be no need to act up and misbehave. When misbehavior does occur it is quickly remedied. His point is that classroom control becomes a struggle as teachers try to make students do uninteresting and irrelevant schoolwork.

The present system of education tends to suck the life out of learning. Students arrive in kindergarten or first grade eager to learn, excited about whatever the next thing is, eyes bright and tails bushy. But somewhere around fourth grade (maybe sooner, in some cases) the eyes begin to dull and the excitement for learning fades. This eventually leads to outright dislike for school by the seventh and eighth grade. (If seventh and eighth graders like school, it is almost always because their friends are there, not because of their learning experience.)

I don't think it is a natural, developmental progression that students come to dislike school. The human brain is a prolific information seeker. Its ability to discover and retain knowledge and skill is staggering. Given the right conditions, our brains will continue to learn and improve right up until we breathe our last breath.

Brains don't turn themselves off; schools turn brains off. It is a potent combination of beliefs and practices that begins to dull the eyes of primary-grades and middle-grades students. Students soon recognize that schools are coercive places. Subject matter is often unengaging and superficial. Students are required to process information at the lowest cognitive level possible through rote recall and memorizing. The subject matter is also divided into separate, individual content areas, usually in 45-minute periods, that are intended to increase efficiency but that in fact rob students of the chance for deeper understanding that comes from considering content areas within the context of each other.

Textbooks encourage coverage rather than depth. Students are faced with getting through the entire book and the idea that everything in the book is important to know. Assessment tends to sort and rank students, rather than guide in improved learning. Further, achievement tests are presented as of great importance, with copies of results going to parents, even though they have minimal connection to what is being taught in the classroom. These are some of the things that dull the joy of learning.

Positive relationships and relevant schoolwork can go a long way toward bringing the joy back into learning, but effective classroom management needs a few more elements for a classroom to run well. I was reminded of this as I listened to a group of students representing grades 7 through 10. They had been asked to talk about what they thought helped classrooms to run better.

"I think it is organization," one girl said rather quickly. "When I think about my experience, I remember teachers who seemed to have their act together. There were procedures for all the main stuff that we did in the room. It really got rid of the confusion." She was on a roll. "I also liked—was kind of surprised, actually—how the teacher didn't get people in trouble for some of the stuff that you usually would get in trouble for. You had to really mess up to get in trouble." She paused a bit. "I just remember having a sense that the teacher knew what she was doing and that we were . . . like . . . safe."

As I listened it sounded to me as though this girl had been in a classroom in which "procedures" and not "rules" were emphasized. Procedures are clear descriptions of how things are to be done in a classroom. Classroom procedures address such questions as:

- What do you do when you first arrive at school in the morning?
- What do you do when the fire alarm sounds?
- What do you do with your assignment after you have finished it?
- What do you do when you finish your work early?
- What do you do when you need to use the restroom?
- What do you do when you have a question?

Procedures are for everyone's benefit and help things to go more smoothly. Things are less confusing when people remember the procedures. All the little details can work out fine when students know what to do.

Imagine how life would be if students knew how to enter the classroom, where to find an assignment (especially where to find it after they had been absent), how a paper is to be done, what to do with it after they've finished it, what to do if they want to sharpen a pencil, and what to do at the dismissal of class. These are just a few of the myriad details in a classroom.

The point, though, is that procedures are different from rules. Rules have consequences, while procedures generally do not have consequences. Students are taught the procedures through review and rehearsal. This rehearsal continues as long as needed. The procedures are posted in the classroom or given to each student as a part of their notebooks. Procedures become routines when students are able to do them automatically. If students forget, they are reminded about the procedure in question.

So much of the traditional fight between students and teacher is eliminated because of an emphasis on procedures rather than rules and discipline. For a very helpful and clear description of procedures, rules, classroom management and more, get Harry Wong's book, *The First Days of School: How to Be an Effective Teacher*. This book is considered a classic by many teachers and parents because of its clear step-by-step approach.

Another student in the group I mentioned earlier, a tenth-grade young man, spoke a bit slower, but his words were marked by thoughtfulness. "I think the attitude of the teacher makes a big difference." Other students around the circle agree with this. "I mean . . . when I say attitude . . . I mean . . . it's nice for teachers to have nice attitudes and to be friendly and all. That's nice, of course. But I'm talking about something more than that." Everybody is really quiet at this point. "I'm talking about . . . I don't know . . . it's like . . . we're trusted, or something. It's like my teacher believes in us." More nodding and agreement around the circle. The young man continues. "The reason I'm kind of saying this is because my family recently moved and when we got to the new place . . . I'm helping to unpack boxes and stuff . . . books actually in the office or study or whatever you call it . . . and I see this little book called *Theory X* or *Theory Z* or something like that. And anyway, I end up looking at a little bit of it . . . , and then I ask my dad about it . . . , since he went to graduate school or something and had to read the book for one of his classes. Anyway, he explains it a bit more . . . , and it's about the idea of bosses or people basically viewing life like . . . other people are basically bad, and we have to help them be good, or . . . other people are basically OK, and we have to help them keep being OK."

His fellow students now have a look on their faces as if they are sitting in the presence of Ghandi or Plato. They're nodding in agreement, but you can tell they are impressed with a classmate who reads something from his dad's graduate program. I was impressed too, since I had read *Theory Z* many years before (in a graduate program) and lo, the kid had basically summarized the book in a sentence. He could have saved me a lot of time if he had been around when I first read the book.

These two students had pointed out two of the most important aspects of preventing behavior problems: seek to have an attitude of trust—believe in students, and create an organized classroom where expectations are not only clearly stated, but even practiced and rehearsed. When these components are combined with meaningful, engaging curriculum, along with an atmosphere based on genuine caring, it really does create a positive classroom environment in which behavior problems are kept to a minimum. Another book that educators and parents will want to consider is *Discipline Without Stress, Punishment, or Rewards,* by Marvin Marshall. He wonderfully describes how the work of discipline begins long before a problem occurs, and describes more fully how a classroom or home can live according to the ideas that have been briefly described in this chapter.

Barbara Coloroso, author of *Kids Are Worth It! Giving Your Child the Gift of Inner Discipline,* thinks that a management plan should be prepared to address the different levels of misbehavior. She describes what to her are the three main levels of misbehavior: mistakes, mischief, and mayhem. She defines mistakes as those things that students do unwittingly, maybe even carelessly, but that need to be kept in perspective.

When two adults are working together and one makes a mistake, the other adult would not think about disciplining or punishing his or her colleague. He or she would talk to the colleague, matter-of-factly point out the mistake, maybe offer a reminder, but life goes on without a federal case being made out of it. Our children and students would benefit a great deal from the same approach. Mistakes should not necessarily be ignored, although some can be, but they should be treated as what they are—simply mistakes. As adults we are often too quick to turn mistakes into a discipline issue, and then we find ourselves in a battle we didn't even want to begin. This is why procedures are so important.

As a superintendent I was visiting a classroom and was talking with the teacher when a student came up and began trying to talk with his teacher too. I backed away, feeling that the student had priority over me at the moment. But the teacher looked at the student and with a hint of a smile asked him, "What's the procedure when I am with a visitor?" The student got a knowing look on his face and quietly moved back to his desk. There was no berating or disgust or even frustration. This was something the class had talked about before, and the teacher was only reminding him of their previous agreement. Nobody was in trouble. A mistake had been made, but it had not been made into a big deal.

What Do You Do When
It Won't Go Away—Dealing With Mischief

Mischief is more purposeful and nagging. It is a cut above the mistakes category, and you can feel it as it is taking place. The behavior may have a bit of a mean streak in it, but not necessarily. In the students' minds they may see the behavior as all in good fun, even if they can admit that the behavior is frustrating to their teacher. In any case such behavior detracts from the learning environment, and in some cases can completely do away with a focus on learning. Instead, the focus is on the mischief as one side tries to outdo the other.

I was walking by the library (the same library in which Trevor and I had visited) after school one day, and as I passed the window in the library door I thought I saw a group of teachers sitting around a table in the far corner. My walking momentum had carried me by the doors, but I stopped and slowly walked backward, retracing my steps, until I could have a better look through that same window. Sure enough, four teachers were sitting at the table, and they were talking about something that, by the look on their faces, seemed important to them. The four of them represented our grades 7-10 departmentalized program.

This was interesting to me. I hadn't called a meeting and I hadn't heard about a meeting that one of them had called. *What could it be?* I thought to myself. My curiosity got the best of me, and I opened the door, entered the library, and headed across the room to where they were sitting. They stopped talking when I entered the room, and as I approached they started to take on a look of sheepishness.

"Hey, guys," I said with an obvious lightheartedness in my voice. "When I saw you in here I couldn't help wondering what wonderful stuff you were working on . . ." The look on my face and the tone in my voice emphasized my curiosity.

Each of them seemed to be waiting for someone else to do the talking. Finally the most experienced teacher of the group spoke up, with frustration in his voice. "These kids are driving us nuts! We're just trying to figure out what to do about it."

Over the next 45 minutes each of them helped me to understand what they were dealing with in regard to student classroom behavior Students, especially in the ninth and tenth grades, just couldn't seem to shut up and get to work. They wouldn't stop talking, and there was a spirit of goofing off that the teachers felt went past normal adolescent behavior. Attempts at talking with them or reminding or negotiating were not working. They were fed up, and they had gotten together to talk about it.

In early August of that school year our entire staff, along with the staff from two other schools, had received the basic week of Glasser's Quality School training. As a staff, we had decided to get the training after reading the book *The Quality School* together with follow-up discussion in staff meetings. So now here we were in early October, and things were not going the way the book described. Part of the teachers' sheepishness might have been because they thought they should be doing better. They had read books, we had talked about Glasser's ideas a lot, and we had received choice theory training. What more could be done?

Another part of their sheepishness might have been because they knew that I believed in choice theory and because they wondered how I would react to their dilemma. It was true that I had read quite a few books, and true that we had talked about these ideas a lot, and true again that we had received effective training. Yet here we all were, not knowing exactly what to do. We had embarked on a journey to become a Quality School, but all of us felt just like the inexperienced teenage driver who revs and revs the engine, only to stall the car when letting out on the clutch.

To make a long story short, we began a project that eventually involved teachers, students, the campus life committee (a subcommittee of the board), and the school board. What came out of the project was a management plan for grades 7-10. The following school year the management plan was included in our school handbook. What follows are those parts of the handbook that refer to that plan. The sections are included as the actual copy appeared in the handbook. I would make some minor changes if I had it to write again, but this way you will get the actual feel for where we were in our thinking and beliefs. The first section shares our key beliefs when it comes to behavior:

Behavior Goals

It is our goal to operate a quality school program in which discipline is not an issue. To that end, our behavior goals are based on the following beliefs:

We believe that—
- Learning increases when there is good behavior.
- Every student can behave well.
- Our success is measured by how well we teach students to be self-managers.
- Our standards for behavior should be those taught in the Bible. Jesus emphasized that we "should love one another," and that we should even "love our enemies." Our behavior should be gracious, kind, patient, and respectful.
- When students misbehave, he or she should be given a chance to "fix" the effects of their misbehavior. This may include the principles of peacemaking as described in Matthew 18.

We were beginning to plant seeds of awareness and understanding in regard to the idea of self-management. We also introduced the idea that people should be given the opportunity to fix what they have broken. Another section commented on a basic overall school approach to classroom management:

Classroom Management

During most of the day students will be in a classroom environment. Each teacher implements a management plan that is appropriate for the age and activity, and will work with students in helping them to become self-managers. Usually this process can be handled within the school program. Parents are kept informed of progress, or lack of it, through phone calls, written reports, or conferences, but for the most part are not expected to solve the problem from the home setting. Students are capable of taking responsibility for their actions and helping to develop a success plan themselves. Occasionally students do need a highly structured program with the school and home working in close connection with each other. When this situation occurs, parents will be contacted and an appointment set up where school and home can communicate and set up a success plan. In some cases, students may not be allowed to return to the classroom until such a conference takes place, or until he or she has developed a plan for fixing the problem. It is important for students and parents to be aware of the classroom behavior goals so that their decisions will contribute to a positive classroom experience for everyone.

This section was significant to us because we were painting ourselves into a corner that we felt was important; that corner was the result of our statement that "for the most part [parents] are not expected to solve the problem from the home setting." Most parents supported this approach and understood its value. A few were upset by what felt to them as a reduction of their involvement, and to be frank, their level of control. The passage was also meant to convey confidence in the students and their ability to solve behavioral challenges or problems. These statements were helpful because they began to explain the thinking and rationale on which the plan was built. Yet, as nice as our thinking was, we still felt we needed to produce the specific plan that follows:

The Classroom Management Plan for Grades 7-10

Classroom atmosphere has an effect on learning. A classroom should be a place in which people respect and care for others, in which talking occurs at the right times and at the right levels, and in which students and teachers are attentive to one another. In simple terms, the classroom is a place in which students stay focused on completing their schoolwork.

When a student is not doing one or more of the above, he or she will be asked to comply. If the student continues to disregard good classroom decorum, he or she will be asked to move to another area of the room. If further misbehavior occurs, the student will be asked to leave class and go to the office or other isolation area. The student's teacher and/or principal will decide whether the student may continue in the regular program. Parents will be informed whenever students are asked to leave a classroom.

After the first request to leave the classroom, the student must make up for that incident, as well as completing any schoolwork that needs to be done, by having an "isolated lunch" at the next lunch period. Student and teacher will confer as to the exact behavior needing to be changed and steps that would be helpful toward accomplishing it.

After the second request to leave the classroom, the student will be required to have an isolated lunch, to stay after school to make up the lost time, and to confer with the teacher. Transportation will be the responsibility of the parent and student. (Students not picked up on time will need to report to the latchkey program.)

After the third request to leave the classroom, the student will have to complete the day in the office and will not be allowed to reenter the school program unless the junior high staff, administration, and campus life committee decide that it is a workable situation. Most likely a conference between the student and appropriate staff will be necessary in order to determine the best decision.

(It should be noted that a classroom management plan is not a complete discipline policy. The classroom plan covers behaviors within the classroom and uses a step-by-step approach. More serious behaviors within or outside the classroom are responded to immediately. Usually when a more serious behavior occurs, a student is placed on in-school suspension until he or she comes up with a plan to "fix" what he or she has done, or has met the discipline requirements of the school staff.)

After reading the actual management plan, some of you might be saying, "Finally, a recipe! Something specific a teacher can actually do." But I would urge caution on thinking that way. What you don't see is the spirit in which we implemented the plan, or the buy-in we sought before ever embarking on the plan. We realized we needed this structure, but we did not want to lose the philosophy of Glasser's ideas or any of the momentum we were beginning to gain. Glasser does say that a school might need a time-out room when it is in the early stages of implementing choice theory. This, in part, is because some students and even some teachers are less able to talk through solutions. Students who have been punished for years are ready for a counterattack on teacher, principal, or parents. It takes a while for some to realize that punishment is no longer seen as the solution, and that they may as well calm down and talk about fixing the problem.

This plan allowed us to stay focused on promoting positive relationships and good instruction, all at the same time. A student who was cutting up was asked or reminded to stop. If he or she kept it up, he or she was moved to another part of the room. If the student still kept it up, he or she was asked to head to the time-out room. The teacher handled each of these steps with a positive attitude. There was no need to threaten or nag. It was all matter-of-fact and friendly. The student would have to be really intent on misbehaving to go through all these steps, yet we did have a few that seemed to test the system. In the end the system worked fine, with no students lost as a result, yet much of the success was dependent on the insights we had gained through reading and training.

For instance, we were concerned about one student in particular as we were about to start the new plan. Mike was a good-natured seventh grader who struggled with being able to stay focused. Some would label him as having attention deficit disorder. We wanted different behavior in the upper-grade classrooms, but we didn't want to get rid of students to achieve it. Mike and I visited about the upcoming plan, and our talk went something like this:

"Mike, I'm a little worried about how you and this plan are going to get along."

"Yeah, I'm a little worried too." He was usually pretty easy to talk with.

"Well, I have an idea that might be helpful."

"What is it? What are you thinking?"

"I am thinking that instead of waiting until the teacher asks you to leave the room after three misbehaviors, you might consider leaving the room, by your choice, after two."

"Huh? How would that help me?" The beauty and logic of the idea evaded him.

"If a student gets officially sent out of the classroom by the teacher, that counts as one send-out. After three send-outs the student is automatically suspended from school."

"I know about that," he said. "How will your idea help me?"

"If you go out after being spoken to two times, then it wouldn't count as a send-out. It would be you realizing that you needed another place to work. You would be deciding what was best for you."

The idea appealed to him, and the teachers thought it was good. All in all, it worked well. Whether it was with Mike or with any of the other students, we didn't want to make them do anything. We just wanted to provide an effective, supportive learning environment. After a send-out the teacher would talk with a student about what had happened and how either one of them could have acted in such a way as to prevent the send-out. Accountability is important.

Some will say that the idea contained an element of punishment, but suspending a student, either with in-school suspension or out-of-school suspension, is not punishment. We needed to know whether the student wanted to be in school and wanted to work with us. He or she needed to know that we were serious about learning. Through it all, through every step of the process, we were friendly and supportive.

Responding to mischief and other purposeful disruptions is easier when we have clear boundaries in mind, and when we explain those boundaries to our students. Engaging, relevant schoolwork is still important. Positive relationships are still important. A matter-of-fact, nonthreatening approach is still important. Yet even with these elements in place some students may still choose to disrupt others. Reasonable boundaries also become important. The temptation to implement boundaries with a coercive spirit becomes very real, especially when we are working with students who display a rebellious attitude, but all of the elements must be implemented with grace and tenderness.

Working Through Serious Mistakes

Coloroso refers to serious mistakes as mayhem, but I refer to them as misbehaviors that are not handled through regular classroom prevention, conferences, or time-outs. Examples of such behavior can include physical harm or threat, extreme acts of defiance or disrespect, dishonesty such as lying or stealing, vandalism, or any other behavior that your school deems serious enough. I am convinced that redemptive management (RM) is the most effective response to serious student misbehavior. RM is based on the idea that students can address what they have done and move on toward better behavior.

RM is also based on supportive adults facilitating a student in working his or her way out of what he or she has gotten himself into. It is important that teachers, principal, or parents not attempt to *make* a student behave a certain way, or attempt to make a student deal with a problem that he or she caused. The school or home can have boundaries, but students need to feel that they are making the choice to make something right and move on. Consequences should be natural or logical, not punitive. Punishment need not be present at this level of misbehavior any more than at previous, less serious levels.

RM is not an exact science. It is based on the idea that everyone needs to be accountable, that people need to be given a chance to address their mistakes, that resources be devoted to helping people address their mistakes when possible, and that punishment need not be a part of a management plan.

When working through a problem at school, teachers and principal need to be supportive facilitators but not the "fixers." This is even more true for parents. Parents need to be interested and supportive, but they shouldn't fight the battle for their student. Students are more than happy to let the adults around them go at it on their behalf, without ever really involving themselves in what really is their own problem. After concluding what misbehavior has actually happened, the student who made the mistake needs to be asked, "Do you want to do better?" and "What are you going to do to address what you have done?"

If the student knows what to do and it is reasonably acceptable, then I would allow him or her to do it, and I would provide whatever support I could in the process. If the student doesn't know what to do or where to begin, then I would coach him or her as much as he or she needed or wanted. I would want to come across with the idea that the student would ultimately choose whether to accept my advice or not, and that he or she would even choose the way to fix the problem, but that I was there to help as much as needed. If he or she refuses to address the problem or has no desire to address the problem, then he or she would not be back in the classroom or school until it was resolved. I would not threaten or get angry.

There are ways that we need to treat each other or treat things, and if serious mistakes are made, they need to be addressed for life to go on as usual. As much as I would want the student to fix the situation, I would not in any way come across in a coercive manner. The school's boundary is that this needs to be fixed. The student would know that he or she is cared for and that the school staff want him or her at the school, but that certain behaviors are not acceptable. At every turn school personnel should come across in a way that says, "Our relationship with you is important to us."

Given that brief description of the basis for RM, I will share a few stories of how it actually works. I have shared the story of Elizabeth and Albert in previous chapters and Trevor's story at the beginning of this chapter, but here are a few more.

Greg's Story

We were having a school picnic at a local park, and we had a number of activities going for the students to enjoy. I had organized a game of J-ball (played on a football or soccer field; it is a combination of soccer, flag ball, and basketball played in such a way that all the participants are involved). There were about 30 players involved, mostly students but some parents too.

The game was going great and people were having a good time, but after a little bit one team started to do better than the other. Greg was on the team that was getting behind. The better the other team did, the worse Greg's attitude became. I could tell how he was feeling and quietly spoke to him about it, but apparently it had little effect.

Shortly thereafter, Greg got the ball after it had been popped into the air and started to run with it (legal in J-ball). He had an angry look on his face, and instead of dodging the opponent in front of him, a smaller seventh grader, he bulldozed right through him and over him, knocking him down. This conduct was certainly a foul according to the rules, but this was worse than a normal foul. It was deliberate, even a bit malicious.

I blew the whistle and asked Greg to sit on the sidelines where he could cool off. He pulled his flag belt off in disgust and headed for the sideline, mumbling as he went. Some of the players attended to the seventh grader, still on the ground and searching for his breath, which had been knocked out of him.

I looked over to the sideline and saw that Greg had not stopped at the sideline but angrily was leaving the area entirely. I called for Greg to stop. He kept going. I called louder for Greg to come back. He kept going. I blew my whistle and called even louder. He continued to ignore me.

In my younger days as a teacher I may have run after Greg, partly because I felt responsible for him and partly because I didn't like to be shown up in front of a lot of people. Fortunately, in this case I did not go after Greg. I got the game going again, but kept an eye on just how far Greg was going. If he had left the area completely, I would have excused myself and followed him, but in this case he never left my field of vision.

Not long thereafter it was time to head back to school, so whistles were blown, materials were gathered, jackets and sweaters were retrieved, and students started to get on the bus. I noticed that Greg was slowly moving back toward the bus as well. I kept loading stuff on the van, having conversations with kids about how their day had gone and how much fun we had had.

Greg actually got in line and was just a few feet from getting on the bus when I asked him to stay behind and help me get the rest of the stuff collected. He groaned and reacted with obvious disgust, but he got out of line and headed out to the field to pick up the goal-line cones. We got everything in the school van, and the two of us headed back to school. It was real quiet almost all the way there. I didn't say anything, and he didn't say anything. As we got closer to school, though, I said, "Greg, I'm disappointed in what happened on the field today." I wasn't upset, and I said it matter-of-factly.

Greg retorted, "The teams were unfair, and you didn't do anything about it! On top of that, you were making terrible calls! What do you expect?"

"Well, we disagree on that. I don't think the teams were an issue, and I don't think the calls were an issue either But even if they were as you say, do you feel that gives you a reason to do what you did to Kevin?"

He huffed as though I had no idea what I was talking about.

"Nothing happened on the field that made it necessary for you to harm another player." He looked out the window in the opposite direction, letting me know that I could say whatever I wanted but that he knew what was really going on.

We pulled up to the school, and he got out of the van and headed through the lobby as though he was going back to class. I said, "Greg, what happened on the field needs to be fixed before you head back to class."

"What are you talking about?" he demanded angrily.

"What happened needs to be resolved. I'm not comfortable with you heading back to class until that takes place." I was still friendly, but my voice had added an element of firmness.

"This is ridiculous," he stated with impressive conviction as he moved toward our staff worship room, which doubled as a time-out room when needed. "How long do I have to be in here?" He figured that he would serve his time and then get on with his life.

"I don't know how long you'll be in here. I want you in your classroom, with your classmates, but resolving this is more important."

Greg huffed again and sat down, disgusted, angry, and seemingly with no intention of addressing his mistake. Right now he needed time to think, and we were fully supportive of him having that time.

Another important point to make here is in regard to set suspension time periods. I am convinced that open-ended suspensions are the most effective. There is no value in students being out of school for one day for doing this or three days for doing that if they haven't had to be accountable for what they did. There is nothing magic in suspension. Several of the students in these stories wanted to know how long they had to be in the time-out room or at home. Each time I was able to say that I didn't know long the time-out would last. It was really up to them.

I checked in with Greg a half hour later, but he still seemed disgusted and angry. I didn't come down on him or tell him he better get his act together. I told him I'd be back later. I was serious about the situation, but I was still friendly and even positive. It was two hours before Greg seemed to soften.

"Look, what do you want? What do I have to do?" He still viewed this as something to make me happy.

"You don't have to do anything. It's up to you whether you want to work on this or not."

There was a pause before he continued. "I'm just too competitive. I acted like a jerk." He looked at me, but I couldn't argue with either of his points.

"Have you thought about what would fix the situation?"

Greg let out an audible sigh and slumped a bit in his chair. "I don't know. I should probably apologize to Kevin." He looked at me again, this time with a hint of hope in his eyes.

"That would be good," I answered. "Anything else?"

"What do you mean?"

"Well, was anybody else affected by what you did?"

"I don't know . . ." He was slumping a bit again.

"When you are around someone who is angry, how do you feel?" I knew that his stepfather was making things difficult for Greg.

"I feel bad. I don't like it."

"There were quite a few people who were out there on the field when you got very angry." Another long pause.

"I . . . I guess . . . I need to make it right with them, too." I could tell that he was beginning to feel the weight of what he had done. He was thinking of the people whom he had affected.

"I think that would be good. Do you need my help?"

"I don't think so. What do you mean?"

"Well, there were quite a few people out there. Do you see yourself talking to them individually or do you see yourself talking to them all at once?"

"All at once?"

"Well, I could get people together if you wanted to do it that way. I have nothing to urge. It's up to you."

He sat there quietly, but I could see the wheels in his head turning. His face revealed the terror that he was considering. Greg could be the life of the party. He was a very intelligent young man, and when he threw that intelligence into his sense of humor, he could be quite funny. It is one thing, though, to cut up in the back of the room and quite another to be on center stage. Greg did not like center stage. I tried not to act shocked when he quietly said, "Well, I guess if you could get people together . . . that would be a help."

With no trace of surprise over the fact that I was about to hear a shy, ninth-grade boy apologize to 20 of his classmates, I said, "I can do that. The period gets out in 20 minutes. I'll get them together then. What about the people I can't get together?"

"Who?"

"There were parents out there that aren't here now." He immediately remembered who I was talking about. Most of them were known pretty well by the students in the school.

Another sigh, but the pause was not as long. "I'll call them."

"That'd work."

At the end of the period I went to the different classrooms and asked the students who had been a part of the game to come to my office for a moment. None of them could have anticipated what was about to happen. When everybody got there, I looked at Greg and said, "I think everyone is here." I then looked at the students crowded into my office and said, "Greg asked me if I would get you guys together in one place. Thanks for coming."

Greg was looking down, but his eyes came up as he was searching for one person. "Kevin . . . I'm really sorry. It was dumb . . . that was dumb. I was angry, and I took it out on you. That was dumb of me." The place was incredibly quiet now. He looked around at the rest of the kids and continued, "I want to apologize to the rest of you, too. I was upset . . . and screwed up."

Voices quickly responded. "Hey, it's OK, Greg" and "We'll be all right." Toby, always able to contribute something to the moment, added, "I don't know if Kevin is going to be all right." Everyone laughed, even Kevin, and even Greg.

As the students filed out of my office I asked Greg to stay behind for a moment. "You OK?" I asked him.

"Yeah, I'm good."

"I just want you to know that you just did one of the most impressive things I have ever seen done in my life. You're a good man." He shrugged his shoulders and tried to mumble it off, but I could tell that the experience and what I said had made an impact on him. There was a renewed optimism in him.

I don't know if I handled Greg's mistake perfectly. I think I might do it differently if I had it to do again. I might have encouraged Greg to do something more than apologize to Kevin. He had physically plastered Kevin, so something more might be in order there.

I didn't make a thing out of his defiance of me as he walked away and ignored me. I had briefly mentioned it during our talk, and he had just as quickly apologized to me. Greg and I were fairly close through our mutual love of basketball, and I could tell that he didn't want there to be a problem in our friendship. But maybe I should have done more there. There is room for improvement, I am sure; but one thing I wouldn't exchange for anything was the way that Greg came to the conclusion that he needed to make things right, and then went about and did it. No punishment could have come close to what he experienced, and what his classmates experienced, and what I experienced.

∞

All fine and good, you might be thinking, but what about a student who doesn't want to fix things? How does redemptive management work then? To help answer these questions the story of Ericka Gale comes to mind.

Ericka's Story

I was out in the school commons area late one morning when Mrs. Benton, our sixth-grade teacher, called me over near her classroom door and explained that she had sent Ericka to the office. Ericka was refusing to do anything she had been asked to do, and something would need to change for Ericka to function in the classroom. Mrs. Benton said that she would explain things in greater detail as soon as she could, but I pretty much had a feel for what had happened. Smaller but similar incidents had occurred with Ericka already this school year, but this one was a bigger deal. Ericka was trying to exist in her classroom by almost ignoring her teacher. I guessed that in her mind she had suffered some injustice or that she was fed up for some reason, and now was going to plant a flag. Whatever flag she had planted, it had worked.

I headed back to the office area and, sure enough, Ericka was in the staff worship room, our time-out area. She had been standing in the doorway checking out what was happening in the lobby area, so she knew I was coming. As soon as I entered the room she moved over to the windows; yet she turned to me and looked me in the eye with a smile on her face.

"Things not going that great?" I thought I would start with something simple.

"Things are going fine." She was still smiling, yet there was something ominous in her demeanor.

"Well, usually people aren't sent out of the classroom when things are going fine. This could be a first, though."

"I hate my classroom, and I hate my teacher." She continued looking at me with the smile, which added an element of eeriness to her words.

"That sounds serious."

"I am serious. I'm tired of her telling me what to do. I'm never going back in there." Still smiling, still looking me in the eye.

So began the Ericka story. The "I'm never going back in there" theme was something that Ericka was adamant about. She had no desire to work things out with her teacher and was seemingly content to remain in the staff worship room. Whenever there were breaks she would stand in the doorway hoping to visit with her classmates when they came by. Within her group, Ericka was something of a hero, even a martyr. In her mind she was standing up for more than just her own needs. She had her classmates to think of, too. Tyranny must be met head-on.

Except there was no tyranny, and Ericka was behaving like a rebellious 12-year-old sixth grader. She was being insubordinate and was angry that she did not have as much control over the room as she wanted. To her, Mrs. Benton stood in the way of that control. I checked in on Ericka throughout the rest of the afternoon, but her feelings were unchanged. We got her books and assignments for her, and she settled in for what appeared like a long haul. Monday came to an end with several of us wondering how we should handle Ericka's resolve.

I visited with Ericka on Tuesday morning and expressed my desire for her to work things out and get back to her classroom. No threats, no frustration, just support. Didn't matter to her, though. She was not going back to that room. I was faced with the very real possibility of Ericka staying in the staff worship room for a long time, maybe the rest of the year. At least, that was what she was saying. Other staff members had known Ericka since she was in kindergarten and had to admit that if any student could make good on a promise to stay in the worship room for the rest of the year, it was Ericka.

I thought about what we as a school wanted and what our boundaries were. We wanted Ericka in her classroom. We wanted to maintain a positive relationship through good times or bad. We realized, though, that Ericka wasn't happy in class and that she was creating an uncomfortable situation for almost everyone around her. Her teacher realized Ericka's strengths and wanted to tap into them, including her leadership ability.

We had no desire to make Ericka do anything. There were no magic words for her to say, no penance to perform. For her to function well in her classroom Ericka just needed to work on resolving the problem. With all that in mind I decided that if Ericka wanted to stay in the worship room for the rest of the year, then so be it.

The following morning I checked in with Ericka as usual. "Good morning, Ericka." The sun was coming in through the windows that served as one entire side of the room. As a time-out area it really was quite pleasant.

"Good morning." Ericka had settled into a more businesslike approach. The smile was not there as much.

"I've been thinking about your situation, and I thought I should talk with you about it." Ericka looked at me wondering what I might have to say. "As much as I want you back in your classroom, you seem firm on not wanting even to work on the situation." Her lips pursed just a little tighter.

"I realize that I cannot make you resolve this, nor can anyone else, for that matter; so it really is your choice as to what you do." I paused because I could tell that Ericka was analyzing every word that I was saying.

"I'd rather you were in your classroom, but you are getting your schoolwork done . . . so if you want to be in here for the rest of the year . . . I've decided that we'll support that and work with you on that. It really isn't what we want, but if that is what you want, we'll work with you." Her words and body language were trying ever so hard to tell me *Fine, that's good news. I'm glad we are all happy about me being in here,* but there was a smidgen of something else that was just now starting to emerge.

From the start we had wanted to remove any feelings of wanting to make a fight out of the situation, but if Ericka had somehow made a fight out of it anyway, what I had just told her left no further room for that kind of thinking. She now understood that whatever she decided was fine with us. I had not begun my visit with Ericka that morning thinking that I was going to call her bluff, but in effect that is what I did. At the beginning of the week, even though we were not threatening her, she was threatening us. She thought there was no way that we would be able to have her in that room for an extended period of time. We decided that we could.

Later that day something else happened that was entirely unexpected. I had been out on campus and was returning to my office. As I entered the lobby I saw a man at the secretary's counter who made my stomach sink a bit. The man was Ericka's father. He did not come around campus that much. I would see him at school programs or at church on weekends, but not more than that. To be honest, he was not very supportive of what we were trying to do at the school. It seemed to me that he was a part of a group of people who were unhappy with the school in general, and with me in particular. And now here he was. His daughter has been on in-school suspension all week, with no end in sight.

As I quickly evaluated the immediate situation, it seemed to me that it might not be that pleasant. I continued to head to my office, knowing that the route there would bring me in direct contact with him. As I approached, he turned and faced me. (I did not realize it at the time, but he was on campus because our tenth-grade teacher had invited him to make a presentation to her class.) I fully expected a confrontation. Instead he said, "I just want you to know how much we appreciate what you guys are doing for our daughter."

He could have said very few things that would have surprised me more than that. I was somewhat speechless, I think. As I continued looking at him, searching for a clue to what was happening, thinking about pinching myself to see if I was dreaming, he continued, "She wouldn't get this at home." I took him to mean that things at home were usually more autocratic. He recognized that she was being given choices.

I returned to my senses and said that we would keep working through this thing together. He said thanks one more time and then headed to the upper-grade classroom for his appointment. As I made my way to my office, still a bit incredulous, I realized that Ericka was more isolated than she realized. The school had taken a reasonable but firm stand, and her parents were appropriately supportive of both Ericka and the school. Both the home and the school were letting Ericka work this out in her way and in her time.

Early on, Ericka had thought we would not be able to keep her in the teachers' worship room all year. She may have thought that this would get her parents even more mad at the school—and now all those pieces were just melting. *Where is a good fight when you need one?* she was probably thinking.

After I let her know that if she wanted to complete the year in the time-out area she could do that, I didn't bring up the need for her to resolve the situation again. I checked on her and made sure she was getting her schoolwork and offered to help with her schoolwork if needed, but I didn't do more than that. On Thursday I could tell that she seemed a bit different, a bit softer maybe. The different staff that came in contact with her treated her with kindness and respect. If she was done with her schoolwork, the secretary even asked if she would like to help her with some jobs. I think it was beginning to sink in that we were really serious about having her in time-out for a long time.

It was Friday morning, almost a full week after deciding to revolt and leave her classroom, that Ericka said she wanted to talk with me. She indicated that she had thought about things, and that she would like to talk with her teacher and see if things could maybe work out better. I acted matter-of-factly about this news and told her I would let her teacher know, all the while projecting an if-that-is-what-you-want reaction.

She knew I was supportive of her decision, but I in no way wanted to portray an "I told you so" or "we won" attitude. As far as we were concerned, this was never about winning and losing. It was about maintaining a positive classroom learning atmosphere, while also maintaining a positive relationship with an unhappy student. It was centered on the student's power to make choices.

Ericka and her teacher had a long visit during lunch (I helped with supervision duties) and Ericka returned to the classroom that afternoon. There was no gloating. Mrs. Benton handled it very well, very lead-manager. Ericka's classmates welcomed her back, and she made it through the rest of the year without further incident.

I think one of the key factors for Ericka was that punishment was never the goal. She knew that, because we were anxious for things to be resolved, and supportive of anything that might be done to help her. The time-out was not a punishment. She didn't want to be in the classroom, and even if she did, her behavior was not allowing her and her teacher to coexist in the room at the same time. The time-out room was pleasant, and people were friendly. She realized that she was going to have to manufacture her anger and resolve on her own each day, because we weren't doing anything to help her in that way.

Rudolf Dreikurs, in his book *Children: The Challenge,* reminds us that "the use of punishment only helps the child to develop greater power of resistance and defiance." Dreikurs and Glasser echo Ellen White in that belief. And I am certain that if we had taken a get-tough approach with Ericka, or Greg, or Elizabeth, or Albert, the stories would have ended much differently. As much as possible we need to take the fight out of the situation. The important thing is not that punishment be exacted, or even that students comply. The important thing is that they recognize what they have done for what it is, and that they make a commitment for wanting to do things better.

❧

Some of the comments and questions I hear when teachers or parents are first learening about a noncoercive approach reveal that most people think that without the element of coercion a classroom or home would be chaos. Without coercion students would do whatever they wanted to do, whenever they wanted to do it. But a noncoercive approach does not mean that at all. My experience is just the opposite. A management plan based on punishment and reward ends up promoting behaviors that are at the very minimum of acceptable standards. A cat-and-mouse game develops, with students and teachers trying to outfox one another. In the end, resentment develops as each side feels the other is trying to gain the advantage, which they are. With a noncoercive approach these elements are completely gone. Rather than focusing on how little has to be done to satisfy the teacher or parent, there is a mutual focus on what truly is best behavior, and if something is amiss, the two parties talk about it and work it out. Accountability is even more present in a noncoercive management plan.

I shared the stories of Greg and Erika, and described in some detail the redemptive management process, because of an incredibly important point that Ellen White makes in the book *Education:* "The true object of reproof is gained only when the wrongdoer himself is led to see his fault and his will is enlisted for its correction. When this is accomplished, point him to the source of pardon and power. Seek to preserve his self-respect, and to inspire him with courage and hope" (pp. 291, 292).

"The true object of reproof is gained only when the wrongdoer himself is led to see his fault and his will is enlisted for its correction." This is the goal. This is what matters. The students I have worked with usually began the process with their eyes down, barely looking me in the eye, but as they began to consider what they needed to do to address or fix the problem their eyes started to come up, and their bearing began to change. I am convinced that our dignity is restored as we get ourselves out of what we get ourselves into.

I do not proclaim these stories as perfect examples of how you should work with your students. I probably have opened myself up to criticism. But whether I worked through these scenarios in a perfect manner or not, my goal was to somehow enlist the student himself or herself for the problem's correction. No other strategy changed my life as an educator and parent as much as that of redemptive management.

This chapter should probably be a book, as I've probably raised more questions than I have answered. The main points that I have wanted to emphasize, though, are as follows:

Classroom management begins with relevant, engaging instruction. This point is so important, yet is almost always overlooked. At every level, from curriculum committees to the teacher making lesson plans for the coming week, educators need to make instructional decisions based on what is good for students.

Classroom management is built on genuine, positive relationships. As part of the human family we all tend to thrive when we are in a friendly atmosphere of support. Teachers need to foster intentional friendships with students and behave as if they like students even when a student is not behaving in a very likable manner. Of greater importance than the relationship between teacher and students is the relationship between and among students. Much attention needs to be given to the ethos of the classroom community.

Teachers need to clearly describe classroom activities or events as procedures, and then rehearse their performance with students. Students are reminded about the procedures and held to the procedures, but when a procedure is forgotten, it is treated as a simple mistake rather than something more.

Classroom rules should be few and well-considered. It is important to have classroom behavioral structure that promotes learning, but this structure or system should be built on the previous italicized components. Problems develop when the structure becomes the focus without regard to relevance of the curriculum, "connected" relationships, and effective procedures. Even when rules are broken, though, punishment is not the goal.

When students make more serious mistakes, the principles of redemptive management should be available to help them address or resolve the mistake. Students learn responsibility and judgment as they are helped to get themselves out of what they get themselves into. Additionally, their dignity and self-worth are maintained, and they come to appreciate the character of God more fully and more accurately.

"The object of discipline is the training of the child for self-government. He should be taught self-reliance and self-control" (*Education*, p. 287).

⌒

A school in which I had been a principal a couple of years earlier asked me to come back and give an afternoon in-service on the Glasser/White correlation. During the presentation I shared the story of Trent. Trent was an excellent athlete who had a problem with not performing well, especially if the team he was on began to get behind. He was a sensitive kid, but was reactionary when his emotions got the best of him. He would begin to get disgusted, then angry; then he would erupt with a verbal shot, or even a physical shot. The physical shot might be an overly aggressive foul during the course of play, but it was always obvious that he had done it on purpose and in anger.

I talked to Trent on those occasions that he "lost it" in a game, but the "losing it" continued. At first I punished him through simple autocratic means, such as "You are out of the game," or "You can't play for a week," but these steps really did nothing to address the problem. I shifted gears and decided to attempt to get to really know Trent as a person, and to talk with him on more than a passing level about this challenge he faced.

I brought up the topic at a time other than when an actual "game crisis" was occurring. Trent was open about his thinking and quite willing to visit. We talked about different possibilities, different solutions to the problem. Together we decided that Trent should not play in pickup games unless I was present or in the area. He knew that I could tell when his attitude was beginning to sour, and he trusted me to let him know when it was time to take a break. Trent also knew, though, that ultimately he needed to be in control of himself. He realized that he needed either to stay in control, regardless of how the game was going, or to take himself out of the game until he was thinking more clearly.

It was at this point in the story that one of the teachers interrupted with a long "Oh-h-h . . . so that's what that was all about." We all looked at her, wondering what "that" was. She continued, "Well, my husband plays basketball on Tuesday nights when the community has the gym, and he told me the other day about this kid—Trent, I guess—who sometimes took himself out of games. He noticed it because it wasn't like . . . quitting the game in disgust, as sometimes is the case. He thought it was like . . . impressive that this kid (he was 18 or 19 by this time) wanted to be in control of himself. I thought it was good, too, even though I didn't know who he was talking about at the time. Now that I know the 'rest of the story,' it really is pretty cool."

I must admit my eyes got a little wet as she related this to us. Our eyes have a tendency to do that when we see evidence of our children or students succeeding in their attempts to be in control of themselves, to gain the mastery, and to become "men and women of usefulness and honor."

CHAPTER **9**

The Relevance Thing

"The great difficulty in education is to get experience out of ideas."—George Santayana.

"Too often we give children answers to remember rather than problems to solve."—Roger Lewin.

I t's sad . . . really." A teacher had hung around after an in-service that I had given and was helping me gather materials and pack up equipment. Most of the other teachers had gone, and it was just he and I organizing unused handouts, taking down large poster papers on which earlier great ideas had been brainstormed, and sorting microphone cords from power cords.

"What's sad?" I wondered aloud as I pulled up a cord that had been taped down to a carpet.

"It's just sad . . ." He was working on putting the data projector away and obviously had something on his mind. "It's sad that we don't learn—that we haven't learned . . . that we have had this information for so long, and that we don't do anything with it. I think that's sad."

"I agree." I affirmed what he was saying, but I don't think he was looking for affirmation or agreement. "That's why I'm sharing this material."

"Yeah, it's good stuff. I just keep getting back to the question. Why, even after getting good material, good stuff, do we keep doing it the way we are doing it? What is it going to take for us—for the system—to change?"

This time he was looking at me and wanted an answer. By the look on his face I could tell that this question was not rhetorical. My mind re-

171

played the day and what we had covered. In fact, as we were cleaning up I was thinking about the last segment of the in-service. For those of you who weren't able to be there I will replay it for you, too.

∽

We had come to the section in which Glasser and Ellen White comment on specific details regarding schoolwork. As a springboard to get things going, I decided to play a short audiotape that a friend had shared with me some months before. The tape was from a conference that he had attended and that he had thought would be of interest to me. The sound was not great, but you could understand the words well enough. Here is what the tape had to say:

"I go into classrooms quite a bit, actually," a man's voice began, "and I have a chance to see what students are producing and what teachers are doing. To be frank, it doesn't look to me that students are producing quality assignments. There are a few in every classroom who do come up with good schoolwork, even excellent schoolwork. But for the most part, students seem not to be engaged in what they are doing. When I examine what students have done, it looks shoddy to me. It looks like they are going through the motions, if even that."

I checked to see if everyone could hear the tape well enough; when the nods indicated the sound was fine, the tape continued.

"Teachers seem to struggle with this, too. They are covering the material, scheduling the classes for their allotted amount each day, but they seem to be going through the motions too. Behavior issues often seem more noticeable than kids doing schoolwork."

There was another voice on the tape at this point. The voice seemed to be asking a question of the person doing the talking, but the second voice was faint. The stronger voice then continued.

"I have thought about what has caused the situation we seem to be in. What has contributed to schools doing things the way they are? I guess I should say we are."

A faint voice can be heard to say "Careful, brother," and then there is general laughter. The clearer voice continues.

"Indeed, I need to be careful because I know that all of us in this room are working hard. We are doing our best. But at what point do we finally ask, Is what we are doing really working? The causes of our situation are complex, to be sure, but it seems to me that a couple of ideas stand out.

There seems to be a general misunderstanding on how people learn. We focus on the act of teaching rather than on what learners need.

This mind-set or approach allows us to, and sometimes even encourages us to, focus on coverage rather than depth. You know, the more-is-less problem. We've got these big textbooks and figure we have to teach everything that's in there. We then become involved in trying to get kids to keep up with the schedule. We end up working on them to make them fit whatever the subject matter happens to be.

"Students realize that we are rushing through topics and come to view the whole process as somewhat of a waste. They figure you have to be in school, but it really isn't relevant to their lives. We ask them to memorize facts and then test them on the information. We give assignments that keep them busy, but beyond being busy, what? On top of that, we assign grades to their performance, even cramming the complexity of their learning into a one-letter grade."

I looked around again to see what the facial expressions would tell me, but the expressions seemed to be withholding judgment so far. I could tell that they were straining to hear what the tape had to say, but that so far they were just focused on listening. The tape continued. "Should students not apply themselves to any of the above steps, we attempt to make them apply themselves."

Another faint voice seems to be asking a question, but one really can't make it out. The clearer voice responds.

"The system of schooling that we have now is based on a model that we have been using for the past 100 years. Between 1850 and 1900—those aren't exact dates, but they are close enough—the idea of 'the common school' was developing to the point where people realized that all children needed schooling. They felt civilization and democracy depended on it. So by the early 1900s schools as we know them were being built to instruct the ever-increasing number of kids.

"The interesting thing is what the schools looked like and the basic premise on which they were designed. At the same time schools were growing in number, industrial breakthroughs were creating a manufacturing explosion. Factories were producing everything from cars to clothes at an astounding pace. The success of the factories had an influence on the design of schools. So much so, in fact, that the similarities were striking.

"Schools and factories in the early 1900s often looked alike from the outside. When you went inside the factory, if it was a clothing factory you would see rows of sewing machines. If you went inside the school next door, you would see rows of desks. In both places efficiency was the goal. Much as cars could be built one piece at a time, it was felt that students' knowledge could be built in the same way. Start with the chassis, add some tires, then some seats, an engine, and so forth. With the kids, start in the first grade, add the necessary knowledge, move ahead into second grade, a little more knowledge, and so on.

"Just as someone decided what the car was going to look like and then created the assembly line to make that car, someone decided what students were going to look like and then created the "assembly line" to make that student. Just as cars were passive recipients as they traveled through the factory, so too were students as they traveled through their schooling years, passively receiving the knowledge and skills that someone else felt they needed."

I pressed the stop button at this point and looked at the faces once again. This time the looks gave me subtle clues as to what they were feeling.

"What do you think?" I asked. "Any comments or questions on what you just heard?" No one had an immediate response, but I was comfortable with the silence that lingered as they considered what they might say. After maybe 15 seconds a voice spoke up.

"Some of my students *do* produce quality." I thought she might say more, but that was it. I think she was trying to say *Give me a break.*

"That's good. It's exciting when our students create something or produce something that reflects quality. And I think our students like it when they produce something of quality. But the question I keep coming back to is this: Do my students, at least the ones who sometimes produce something of quality, do they produce quality *because* of me or *in spite* of me?"

Some nods of agreement rippled through the audience.

I elaborated. "Some students are really interested in certain areas, or maybe they come from a home that is highly supportive. I remember giving an assignment to a seventh-and-eighth-grade class one time; one of the students fulfilled the assignment by bringing an eight-foot wind tunnel to the classroom. It was made of see-through plastic of some sort and had a fan at one end. She had created wings of different shapes and sizes that fit into a slot in the midsection of the tunnel. When the fan was turned on, the wings would rise at different speeds and to different heights, based on their unique lift design. It was quite impressive.

"Another student in the same class, having received the same assignment, brought a large shoebox with some plastic figures inside, in which he was trying to create a panorama. It was extremely simple in nature, something that a second or third grader might make without help.

"As I thought about it, though, I realized that the student who brought the wind tunnel was a gifted student from a gifted home. I didn't doubt that she had done the work, and she could certainly describe everything about her project. But her home was like Leonardo da Vinci's workshop. Her dad was an incredible person of skill and insight, and she had tapped into his interest as much as she had her own.

"The second student, on the other hand, came from a very difficult situation in which he was totally on his own. Not only was he on his own; he needed to deal constantly with dysfunctional challenges that faced him every day. In the case of the wind tunnel, I had to admit that other than giving the assignment I had done nothing to draw that quality out. In the case of the panorama project, I had to ask myself what I had done to help that student. What had I done to teach him or coach him?"

"But aren't students supposed to be responsible for their own learning?" a teacher blurted.

"That is our goal," I replied. "We want students to take more responsibility for their learning, but we can't forget that taking responsibility takes skill and know-how. Kids can be only as responsible as we have taught them to be." The facial expressions throughout the room let me know there were still questions on this point. "The act of learning depends on how we set up the classroom. It depends on the kind of freedom and power that we give students. It depends on our system of accountability."

"Such as grades?" another teacher interrupted.

"Grades are usually a part of our system of accountability."

"I hate the way we do grades now," she continued. Many nods of agreement and sounds of affirmation were projected by those sitting around her.

"Glasser would agree with you," I responded. "He feels the present system of grading is destructive."

It felt as though the teachers were especially interested in this point. There were other opinions, though, and one of those views now spoke up. "What's wrong with grades? I hear the complaints, but you've got to have grades, don't you? I mean, kids have to know how they are doing." Several nods of agreement could be seen around the room.

"Well, that's a good point. Let me ask you a question. Do grades help students learn?" It became quiet as everyone seemed to be thinking on how they would answer it.

A teacher who hadn't spoken to this point now added her opinion.

"To tell you the truth, I don't think grades, at least the way we give them, help students learn." Many sounds and nods of approval responded to her comment. "We let them know how we think they did, but that really doesn't help them learn anything."

"Well," I said, "that's the rub, isn't it? The question that keeps coming back to me is, and I think this is of incredible importance, Are we teaching or are we sorting?" A real quiet settled on the group at this point. "Because it seems to me that when we give assignments and then give a grade at the end of the assignment we are merely sorting the students according to how they were able to complete it. That doesn't seem all that noble or even helpful. The skill is in helping all of the students get over the bar of competence or better. Feedback that we give them should assist them in their learning; otherwise, I think the feedback is more for us, the adults in their lives, than it is for them."

"So what do we do?" a voice asked from near the back row. Sounds of agreement rippled around the room.

"It seems that we are in agreement that we could use help in this area. So let me say two things—one, this would be a great point to begin going through the slides comparing what Glasser and Ellen White have to say regarding academics and schoolwork . . ."

"Yeah, let's see what you've got."

". . . and two, before we are done here I will share an example that I think will answer your specific question regarding how evaluation can be helpful. The example has really clarified things for me, so I will share it before we leave today. Let's look at the first slide."

"A quality school would not accept low-quality work from any student" (*The Quality School*, p. 97).

"This is one of Glasser's foundation points. If a topic or assignment is worth asking the students to complete, then it should be worth them putting their best effort into it. When we accept shoddy work that doesn't reflect effort, we send the message that the value of the material we are covering is not that great. Glasser feels that a grading strategy that allows students to get C's and D's and still pass sends a message that mediocrity and incompetence are good enough. And over time it affects the degree to which the students see themselves as capable people. If we don't expect them to be competent, and consistently convey that, why should they see themselves any different? Some react to Glasser's ideas regarding classroom behavior and learning with skepticism. They hear him saying that punishment and grades as we know them should be done away with and they figure that behavioral and academic chaos will be the result. Actually, such strategies have the opposite effect."

At this point in the seminar I probably should have said more about this "opposite effect." I should have explained how a competency-based classroom operates, and how students can produce amazing results when three things are in place: (1) positive, supportive classroom relationships; (2) engaging, useful schoolwork; and (3) helpful assessment that includes the element of self-evaluation. But I didn't. Instead I put up the next slide:

"I have been struck with how little depth there is to what the students are assigned to do as individuals. There is credence to the complaint of students that school is boring and I believe that the basis of this complaint is that they find it superficial" (*Control Theory,* p. 72).

Schools are under constant scrutiny, and teachers are frequently second-guessed, so I am aware of the need for sensitivity when giving in-services. Glasser and White have important points to make, though, and sometimes the slides have to tell it like it is. I continue in a matter-of-fact manner. "The opposite of depth or going deep into something is staying on the surface or being superficial. A superficial approach to curriculum allows us to cover a lot of topics without going deeply into any of them. Somehow we forget that there is no way for anyone to learn everything there is to know on even one topic, never mind several topics.

"Take just one area—history, for example. Think of all the history that has occurred since the beginning of time. Is it our goal to attempt to teach all of it? No, you say, that would be ridiculous. So, what then? What do we teach? Or better said, What do we want students to learn? It becomes clear that our goal is twofold—(1) we want students to understand certain events in history because of the bearing those events can have on our thinking and on our circumstances today, and (2) we want students to learn how to learn. We want them to possess the curiosity and the skill of the researcher. We want them to understand the decisions of the past and how people struggled with those decisions. We want them to recognize the true heroes, especially the unsung heroes who made a difference in the absence of fanfare and popularity."

The group seemed to be with me. I felt they could tell that I understood the challenge of teaching. "And so we must be wise choosers of the topics into which we will go deep, and by going deep students will not only come to understand what others before them have struggled with, but they will also become skilled, ongoing learners themselves. Ellen White wanted to give us permission to employ this approach as well."

"God has given inquiring minds to youth and children. . . . [Teachers] should not be satisfied with doing surface work" (*Fundamentals of Christian Education,* p. 368).

"The schoolroom is no place for surface work. No teacher who is satisfied with superficial knowledge will attain a high degree of efficiency" (*Education,* p. 278).

"It seems clear," I continued, "that Glasser and Ellen White view the idea of depth as important, although they are not unique in this area. Many other current educational authors and researchers are saying the same thing. What is of interest to me, though, is that Ellen White was emphasizing depth during a time when others were emphasizing efficiency and coverage. She was encouraging teachers to get in the habit of going deeper."

The point was made, I thought, and there were still a number of slides to go over. "OK, depth, whenever possible, is the goal, and superficial coverage is the opposite of depth. Let's look at an example that Glasser feels pretty strongly about when it comes to superficial schoolwork." I put up the next slide.

"Busywork is the epitome of low-quality schoolwork" (*The Quality School,* p. 89).

I let everyone read the words and reflect on what they meant for them personally. I shared a few ideas, though. "Having students complete assignments because it will fill time, or even because they need review, doesn't result in quality."

"What do you mean, reviewing doesn't result in quality?" There was some frustration in the man's voice, but not a serious amount.

"Good question. I don't mean to say that review is bad. What I do mean to say is that having students complete 40 math problems may not have the effect that we think. Students who know how to do the problems will do them correctly, resenting the last 30 of them because of the needless redundancy. The students who don't know how to do them will do 40 of them incorrectly. It would be better to require five problems with students describing each of the steps they are taking in the process." Heads nodded in agreement. "I'm only suggesting that there is a difference between effective review and ineffective review that really is more busywork than anything. OK?" Most seemed to agree, and I moved on. "This next slide is interesting."

" 'Boring' usually meant that we could not relate what we were asked to do with how we might use it in our lives. For example, it is deadly boring to memorize facts that neither we, nor anyone we know, will ever use except for a test in school" (*The Quality School,* p. 7).

"I found this interesting because as educators we often connote memorization with rigor. We want to make learning challenging, and having students memorize things is a way to do that. Except that Glasser points out that such an approach actually has the opposite effect. He allows that some students can and do memorize, but he quotes a wonderful insight from the gifted cartoonist Charles Schultz, who pointed out in one of his *Peanuts* cartoons that "the difference between an A student and an F student is that the A student remembers the information until five minutes after the test and the F student remembers it until five minutes before." Much laughter ensues, and everyone seems to relate to this truism. I let it settle down before continuing. "It really jumped out at me when I discovered the following from Ellen White. Again, remember not just what she is saying, but when she is saying it."

"For ages education has had to do chiefly with the memory. . . . Students have spent their time in laboriously crowding the mind with knowledge, very little of which could be utilized" (*Education,* p. 230).

"Education has consisted in laboriously loading the minds of students with material which cannot be of the least value to them" (*Fundamentals of Christian Education,* p. 397).

"Instead of burdening their memories with an array of names and theories that have no bearing upon their lives, and to which, once outside the schoolroom, they rarely give a thought, let them study all lands in the light of missionary effort and become acquainted with the peoples and their needs" (*Education,* p. 269).

I put these up one at a time so that they could have a good chance to consider the ideas fully.

Heads are shaking, and it is obvious that the quotes have struck them with the same clarity with which they struck me. "It's pretty clear here, isn't it?" People nod in affirmation. "Glasser emphasizes the need for learning to be useful, and Ellen White emphasizes it just as strongly. Glasser points out that there is a danger of teachers focusing on irrelevant material that 'cannot be of the least value' to students; so does Ellen White."

A hand goes up slowly, and I ask the man to share his question or comment. He begins at the same speed his hand went up, but while slow and thoughtful, he speaks so that all can hear him. (You know how quiet people get when quiet people are speaking.) "Well . . . the timing of this in-service is interesting to me." He pauses, which adds to the effect on everyone, straining to hear each word. "It's just that I have been thinking of some of these very things for the past few months. I really want to make a real difference in my students' lives . . . and I wonder if what I do . . . the way I teach . . . if it makes that kind of difference."

He pauses and looks around to see how people are reacting. His fellow teachers, including me, agree that they know exactly what he is talking about. "I give tests, but then I wonder if the tests really tell me much about what the kids know. Some of the kids do well on tests, even if they don't read and study. Other kids don't do well even when they do study. I think about Ellen White talking about students becoming thinkers and not mere reflectors of other people's thoughts, and I wonder if my kids are becoming thinkers. I mean, that is what we are talking about, isn't it?" He looks at me, along with all the other people in the room.

"Yes," I say, "that is pretty much what we are talking about."

He continues. "I mean, so much energy and time is put into trying to figure out exactly what score kids have, but what I really want to know is Do the kids understand? What evidence can they give me that they understand?" His fellow teachers agree. "Beyond understanding, I really like it when students are deeply interested in a topic. Somehow, the way we teach—well, it just seems to deaden understanding and kill interest."

He made his points well and summarized things in a better way than I could have, and I told him so. I added that what he shared "was a perfect lead-in to the next slide, which focuses on what students need for good learning to take place."

"Three basic requirements for a good education are involvement, relevance, and thinking" (*Control Theory,* p. 115).

I ask the teachers to "think about what each of the three key words mean. Involvement suggests a team effort between teacher and students, where students are involved with every step of their education, including the planning before the lesson and the evaluation afterward. Relevance stresses the need for usefulness. Students need to be involved with material that means something to them. Our challenge is creating that connection. And thinking implies intellectual struggle or 'grappling,' as Theodore Sizer puts it."

At this point I had to put in a plug for Sizer. "Ted Sizer is a resource with whom I think you will want to become familiar. His book entitled *The Students Are Watching* contains a chapter on grappling and is an excellent book on ethics and morals in education. It is written in a very easy-to-read format, but is a 'deep' read, nonetheless. I should tell you, too, about his book entitled *Horace's School,* which contains a section on the kinds of learning that we should be having kids memorize. *Horace's School* was an inspiring read to me."

"How do you spell Sizer?" someone asks.

I give them the information, and even go to one of my storage cases and pull both books out for people to examine as we continue. "Glasser summarizes things pretty well on this next slide," I say as I put it up on the screen.

"It will take time to realize that teaching is not doing things *to* or *for* students: Teaching is structuring your whole approach in a way that they want to work to learn" (*Control Theory*, p. 79).

"We've talked about the importance of relationships," I point out, "and we have talked about the need to get rid of coercive practices, but we also need to apply these principles to our instructional planning. Some of us might not think it is possible for students to want to learn, but I think it is. And ultimately, if they don't want to learn, then we are right back into the cat-and-mouse games of coercion and compliance. So we need to buy into this paradigm, this approach to learning."

"Easier said than done," a voice quietly pointed out.

"No doubt about it—much easier said than done," I agreed. "But what is the alternative?"

"I experience the alternative on most days, and frankly, I'm a little tired of it," another voice admits.

"Well said," I affirmed. "Check out this next slide."

"Children go through the routine of study mechanically, but do not retain that which they learn. Many of these constant students seem almost destitute of intellectual life. The monotony of continual study wearies the mind, and they take but little interest in their lessons; and to many the application to books becomes painful. They have not an inward love of thought, and an ambition to acquire knowledge. They do not encourage in themselves habits of reflection and investigation" (*Fundamentals of Christian Education*, pp. 26, 27).

"I know this is what we want," I say after giving them time to read the statement. "We want our students to love thinking and to enjoy striving for knowledge. The question keeps coming back, though: How do we structure classrooms—indeed, how do we structure learning—in such a way that students understand the value of reflection and investigation? How do we create that 'want' in them?"

At this point it hits me that, for the most part, the group of teachers that I am talking to *understands*. They understand what Glasser and Ellen White are describing. They understand what the future of education needs to look like. I decide to alter my approach for the last few slides. "There are a few more slides," I explain, "but I want to do things a little differently as we close. I will put a slide up, but instead of my commenting on what it says I would like one of you to make clarifying or summarizing comments. Can you handle that?"

"Bring it on," a voice challenges. Teachers are such a wonderful breed.

"OK, here's the first slide."

"Instructors should endeavor to surround [students] with objects of the most pleasing, interesting character, that the mind may not be confined to the dead study of books" (*Fundamentals of Christian Education,* p. 322).

I give them a little time, and then I suggest, "Share with the person next to you on how you might comment on this quote." After a couple of minutes I invite someone to share with the larger group.

A hand goes up slightly, and a teacher, whom I don't think has spoken yet, offers her insights. "Well, it seemed to us (she acknowledged her partner at this point) that it was a warning of sorts to be careful of depending on books, such as textbooks, too much. But it seemed to be saying more than that, too. We both have been doing quite a bit with multiple intelligence activities, you know, where you create learning that touches on all nine of the main intelligences."

I am impressed. "Share more about that. What did you and your partner come up with?"

She seems a little shy now that I have put her on the spot about a specific idea, but she wades in admirably. "Well, including learning activities that allow students to work in different areas than the usual 'writing out answers' mode really does create an atmosphere of greater interest to them. Having them complete assignments using their art skills, or their music skill, or their interpersonal skill, really draws on their thinking ability and adds life to a potentially boring lesson."

"Thank you both. That is an excellent example and a helpful summary. Let's try the next slide."

"The teacher should carefully study the disposition and character of his pupils, that he may adapt his teaching to their peculiar needs" (*Counsels to Parents, Teachers, and Students* p. 231).

"Share with a different partner this time. I'll give you a couple minutes." The partner share format is a good way to get everyone in the classroom involved, and takes very little time to get into or get out of. After two minutes I break into the many conversations buzzing across the room. "Who will share their thoughts on this slide?"

"I'll take a shot at it," an experienced male teacher offers. "A number of things impressed us about this short passage. It seems to be reinforcing what we have been considering throughout the day—the idea, for instance, of a noncoercive, relationship-based approach; the idea of the teacher knowing his students so well that he could tailor his teaching to the students' interests and skills; the idea of the teacher working to adapt the material to the learner, rather than the learner to the material. Those were a few of our ideas."

"Wow!" I exclaimed. "That is some great work for the short time you had to discuss it." Everyone else in the room agreed with my appreciation for their response.

"We also agreed with what was previously said regarding a multiple intelligence approach. Our passage seemed to affirm that as well."

"I feel that I shouldn't even ask this question, since their comments seem so complete, but I'll risk it. Does anybody have anything to add regarding this last quote?"

A man started talking without raising his hand. "I was reading recently—I can't remember the author—but anyway, he was talking about how we—teachers, that is—need to be students of our students." People around the room were slowly appreciating the deeper meaning of what he was saying. "That's what Ellen White is describing, the idea that we study the real makeup of our students. Our students might be studying their schoolwork, but we are studying them."

"That is such a great insight, such a neat way of helping us to better understand what Ellen White was saying. I'd love to know where you read that."

"Yeah, I would too." Light laughter surrounds us in quick response.

"Let's keep going. Here's the next slide."

"Before attempting to teach a subject, [every teacher] should have a distinct plan in mind, and should know just what he desires to accomplish. He should not rest satisfied with the presentation of any subject until the student understands the principle involved, perceives its truth, and is able to state clearly what he has learned" (*Education,* p. 234).

"I'll give you a little more time on this one. Get in groups of three to discuss what you think are the main ideas." The group seems used to the drill by now, and triads quickly form and begin to compare thoughts and inspirations. (In a classroom setting I would organize the groups or form them randomly.) After three or four minutes I say "Ready or not, here I come," and then add that I would like to do things a little differently for this quote. "I would like each triad to count off in threes. I have chosen a number between one and three, represented by the fingers I am hiding behind my back. I will select a triad randomly and then show you the number behind my back. That person will be the lucky presenter."

There are some groans and playful "Oh, great"s, but everyone quickly gets a number. "OK," I say after a short time, "are we ready?" I look around the room slowly and dramatically, and finally select a triad toward the back. They respond appropriately, as though I have just chosen them for a life-threatening mission. But they still don't know which of them will be chosen as presenter. I don't know which of them is number one, two, or three, but I slowly pull my hand out from behind my back to reveal two fingers. It is immediately obvious which of the three has chosen the number two. She looks at her triad partners with a grin, and then at me, and then figures she might as well share what they talked about.

"We felt that one of the obvious ideas was the need for planning. We really need to know where we are going before we begin. I know that I enjoy my teaching so much when my planning is in order. We noticed the word 'understands,' and it reminded us of what we have been talking about this afternoon. Understanding really is the goal. And we noticed the phrase 'able to state clearly what he has learned.' We talked about ways that we ask our students to state what they know, and how when we simply give a test over material that we have covered we wonder if we have really given all of the students a chance to reveal what they know. Some kids are good test takers. Anyway, you know what I am saying."

"I think we do. Thank you; you have pulled out some key points. And you presented them even after being put on the spot." Some quiet laughter. "Well done. Let's do two more slides, and everyone keep their number. We'll use that method again. Here's the next quote."

"The use of object lessons, blackboards, maps, and pictures will be an aid in explaining these lessons, and fixing them in the memory. Parents and teachers should constantly seek for improved methods. The teaching of the Bible should have our freshest thought, our best methods, and our most earnest effort" (*Education,* p. 186).

Time is given for the groups to discuss the slide. After similar fanfare a triad is chosen, along with the presenter. The lot has fallen on a young primary-grade teacher, but she is determined to represent her triad well. "H'mm, well, we kind of saw three almost separate ideas. The first is her emphasizing the need for us to be cutting edge, you know, as modern as possible. In her day, blackboards, maps, and pictures were cutting edge. If she were writing today, she would probably be talking about computers and distance learning.

"Then we saw her emphasizing the idea of always striving to do better. I hear fellow teachers in my school talking about learning strategies that are 'best research/best practice.' I think she was a best research/best practice person herself." I find myself really appreciating what she is saying, along with everyone else. "Finally, we were impressed that of all the classes that need our best effort, our best resources, and highest creativity—it is Bible class. That really struck us."

A number of groups said, "Us too."

"OK, last slide."

"So long as the great purpose of education is kept in view, the youth should be encouraged to advance just as far as their capabilities will permit. But before taking up the higher branches of study, let them master the lower" (*Education,* p. 234).

I had selected a triad made up of some of the teachers who earlier in the day had come across as more skeptical, and wouldn't you know it, the lot fell on Mr. Skeptical himself. He chuckled when it fell to him, somehow seeing the irony in his having the last word, so to speak. He looked at me for a few pregnant moments, as if to ask, "Do you really want me to have the floor?" But I was quite comfortable with him in that position. I wanted to hear what he had to say.

"Well, before I share what we talked about, I just want to say that I have appreciated this day and what we have covered. I've got some real stuff to think about." Skeptic or not, he was a gentleman. "A couple of things hit us from this passage. First, we were reminded of one of the slides this morning in which Ellen White talked about its not being really wise to confine students to certain grades, because kids learn at different rates. It hit us that our system of grades may actually artificially hold students back, such as 'We can't cover that now because you are going to learn that next year.' The grades are more for us, the adults, than they are for them." Noises of agreement ripple across the room.

"The other thing was the idea of mastery. We have talked a little bit about that today, but it hit us that Ellen White probably would agree with Glasser when it comes to grading. For students to master something before going on to the next step is more important than giving students a C or a D and then passing them on. The more I think about that, the more I am amazed at how long we have been doing it. In general, kids are striving to go as high as we expect them to go, which often isn't very high."

I look at him for a few quiet moments, my eyes conveying my appreciation for his grace and his candor. "Thank you; well said. The mastery thing is huge, and we need to talk about it; but it will have to be at another time, since our time is about up."

"You said you were going to share some excellent example of mastery in action, or some cool evaluation idea before we left," a voice declared from somewhere over on the left side of the room. "Yeah," other voices agreed.

"I did, didn't I? Well, that would be a good story to end this section on. Consider the following scenario. An eleventh-grade teacher assigned a research paper, usually a daunting task. Now, some students are able to complete a research paper competently, but most really don't know how to write such a paper very well, and some students have virtually no idea where to begin. In a traditional setting the teacher would give the assignment and then give the students time to complete it. After the papers are turned in, the teacher would grade the papers and whatever the student got, then that's what he or she gets.

"In an average classroom with 20 students, how many of the 20 do you think could do well writing a research paper? I'm thinking maybe four of the 20 doing really well; maybe another six to 10 doing a passing job; with the rest, maybe six to 10 students, having no clue where to begin. This classroom I am going to tell you about, though, was not a traditional classroom.

"After giving the assignment, this teacher handed to each student an example of an exemplary research paper that had been turned in some time before, with the name of the writer hidden. She asked the students to read the paper and to think about the elements of the paper that made it exemplary. She then put the students in small groups and had them identify the things in the paper that made it great. The ideas were shared among the larger class and written on the board.

"Next, the teacher handed out an example of a shoddy paper, again with name hidden, and had the students go through the same steps, this time identifying the things that made the paper shoddy. With all the suggestions and points on the board, the teacher and students refined them into seven major areas that should be kept in mind when writing a research paper. It was only after this process had been completed, a process that took several days, that the teacher gave the students permission to begin on their own papers." There are looks of support and interest as teachers consider the implications of this approach.

"What do you think? Do you think that students would do well on research papers with that approach?" Lots of agreement. "It's interesting, because with the mastery rubric set before the students even started—a rubric that they helped to set up—each of them became capable peer assessors. In other words, because they could see the target they could tell how they themselves were doing, and could help classmates hit the target as well. It has been said that students can hit any target that we set up and hold still.

"This story is an example of how assessment and instruction can be so closely aligned that you can hardly tell the difference between the two. Evaluation doesn't have to be something that just comes at the end of the lesson. Evaluation is best when it starts at the beginning, continues through the middle, and stays on through the end of the learning."

That evening I returned home and was going through the written evaluations that teachers had given me. One teacher wrote, "What an amazing day! So much to think about. I had heard of this Glasser fellow before today, but now my curiosity is really piqued—I will check out some of his stuff right away. I was pleasantly surprised to see an adversary from my past (I guess adults in my life misrepresented her or something)—Ellen White—in a new light. Quite a woman. What you and Glasser and Ellen White are saying needs to be said. We are slow to catch on, but don't give up on us. If what you are saying is true, the end result will be worth the wait and the effort. Courage."

As I read the note a sense of thankfulness came over me. I was thankful that she took the time to write a message of encouragement, but more than that, I was thankful that she understood. I think I am like most teachers when it comes to such thankfulness. There may be pressures and expectations for teachers to be concerned with traditional types of grading and standardized test scores, but I am convinced that there is no greater satisfaction for a teacher than when students understand.

As we put the last few boxes of materials into the back of my car he thanked me for a good day, and I thanked him for all the extra help he had given me. More than that, I appreciated the fact that I had made a new friend. We expressed our desire to stay in touch in the future. As I headed out of the parking lot and turned toward home I reflected on the question he had thought aloud to me earlier. "I just keep getting back to the question," he had said, "of why, even after getting good material, good stuff, we keep doing it the way we are doing it. What is it going to take for us—for the system—to change?"

What do you think?

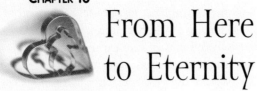

CHAPTER 10

From Here to Eternity

"The whole purpose of education is to turn mirrors into windows."—Sydney J. Harris.

Recently I presented a breakout session at the CAPSO Convention in southern California. CAPSO stands for California Association of Private School Organizations and is made up of private schools from around the state, many of them parochial. My topic was on comparing Glasser's ideas to the ideas found in Scripture. This book has focused on the comparison between the Spirit of Prophecy and Glasser, but Ellen White herself referred to her writings as the lesser light and continually encouraged us to go to the greater light for the ultimate answer to our questions.

Even more important than where Glasser's ideas stand in relation to Ellen White's is where they stand in relation to those of such men as Moses, Ezekiel, Paul, and especially Jesus. I have found it fascinating to read the Bible with the principles of choice theory in mind. Over time I have collected a significant number of biblical stories and texts that speak to Glasser's ideas, and when I proposed the topic to the CAPSO organizers they accepted the proposal.

With approximately 125 schools throughout the state, Seventh-day Adventist schools comprise a significant part of CAPSO. More than 3,000 private school educators attended the convention, but almost 1,000 of those were Adventist educators. Many of the people who attended my breakout session were fellow Adventists, most of whom I recognized, having lived and worked in our church educational system for 25 years. Some may have attended because of a close personal friendship that we enjoyed, but most were there because of a growing awareness and interest in Glasser's ideas. As I have said, there is something deeply spiritual in the principles of choice theory and the Quality School. About half of those in attendance, though, represented schools from other faiths, including Roman Catholic and Lutheran.

I shared what I had collected on Glasser and the Bible and then allowed time for questions or comments. One woman toward the back asked a question that I wasn't sure I totally understood, but I began an attempt at answering it when a woman to my right got my attention and asked if she might comment. I was happy to give her the floor, in part because I didn't feel that I was doing that great with it anyway.

As she started talking, though, I wondered if she was going to say something that would support what I had presented or disagree in some way. Very quickly I realized that she was going to be a big help. She affirmed what I had been trying to say, which made me feel good; but when she said that she had recently taught at the Huntington-Woods Elementary School in Michigan, that got the attention of several of us. To people who know much about Glasser the words Huntington-Woods are very significant. This elementary school was the first Glasser Quality School in the United States. A number of training videos have been filmed at the school. Educators from around the United States and the world travel to Wyoming, Michigan, to see choice theory in action. When this teacher mentioned the words Huntington-Woods, she became "E. F. Hutton" to several of us.

For those at the breakout session who may not have known about how special this school was I gave a quick description of what they had accomplished. Our eyes then went back to this teacher, who proceeded to tell us a little bit about herself. She had taught at the primary-grade level and loved working at the school. She confirmed that the school was everything the videos said that it was, which shouldn't be too surprising, since one of the traits of a Glasser school is that it will be a place that both teachers and students enjoy coming to.

But her husband was a Lutheran pastor, and he had recently accepted a call to the West Coast. She now found herself working in a new school that knew nothing about choice theory or Glasser's ideas. She admitted that it was a difficult transition for her, that at times she wrestled with discouragement. Imagine working at a school that embodied what has been described throughout this book, only then to have to go to another school that operated from the usual boss-management approach. It would be hard.

When she arrived at the convention, she was curious about the breakout on Glasser and the Bible, something that she had given some thought to, but not at any length. She shared that the breakout had been an encouragement to her and that realizing just how closely aligned choice theory was with Scripture had reenergized her.

After the breakout she lingered behind and visited with people. When most had left for the next breakouts on the schedule, she approached me as I was putting the last cords in the projector case.

"I am so glad you were here today," I said.

"I am too," she replied.

"It's amazing," I continued, "how God brings people together or brings them to events that are important to them, or to the event."

"I agree."

"In this particular case," I pointed out, "you really added to the significance of the breakout." Moments can suddenly become very special, and she had created that kind of moment at the end of the presentation.

"Look," she said, "I appreciate what you are saying, but I need to ask you a question."

I could tell she was serious about something. "What's that?" I wondered aloud.

"Where are you going with this?" Her eyes were locked on mine, and it was clear that this was more than a question.

She remained quiet as I searched for an answer. "Well, I'm really not sure." She still remained quiet, somehow conveying that my answer was not good enough. I continued, "You know, I discovered some of these correlations, and I figured I would let people know about it." My answers were not gaining in power or credibility.

"It appears," she continued after slightly shaking her head, "that you may not fully understand the value of what you have shared today. You need to know where you are going. It's too important to have this be just another breakout—just another in-service." There was a short period of quiet. "I just want to let you know that I appreciated what you shared, and I want to encourage you to keep at it. It's good news."

∽

In my journey toward seeking to understand the principles of William Glasser and how they relate to the principles of morality, life, and eternity, there are two questions that stand out in my mind. They are more like events than questions. The first one occurred years ago, in that school multipurpose room, during a parent workshop, when one of the parents pointed out that "I don't know why we have to go to secular authors when we have the 'red books.'"

How frustrated I was at the time over this attitude, said when it was said, in the place it was said. Yet that question, that event, changed my life and started me on a quest that just keeps expanding. How wonderful are God's ways and methods. In answer to that question/statement, I would say that it is true that the red books do have what we need. And it has been within their pages for more than 100 years. Yet we have missed the point. Who knows the reason? Maybe we have read Ellen White's ideas from a certain perspective or paradigm and that perspective has diminished the crucial point. Maybe our familiarity with her phrases and views has caused us to overlook the deeper message. Whatever the reason, the ideas of a secular humanist are alerting us to the gold mine on which we have been sitting.

I recently read the chapter in *The Desire of Ages* entitled "We Have Seen His Star." This chapter describes how the religious leaders of Israel had access to the Old Testament scrolls for centuries and were knowledgeable regarding the messianic prophecies, yet it was the visit of the Wise Men from the East that aroused Jerusalem's attention to the birth of Jesus. Sometimes God conveys a message from many different angles to make sure that we don't miss it. He is generous in that way. Glasser probably does not view himself as a wise man from the East (although he was born in Cleveland), yet it seems that he has alerted us to ideas that we have had at our disposal all along. We have had Ellen White's insights on education and schools for more than 100 years.

The other question that seems incredibly significant—I think even more significant than the first—is that from our Lutheran friend at the CAPSO convention: Where are we going with this? Glasser has helped many, many people through his ideas on how to take responsibility for our lives, including how we think. He has helped many, many teachers and students to make schools a place of relevance and meaning. Imagine the impact these principles of living could have if supercharged with the blessings of the Holy Spirit.

Seventh-day Adventists are not alone in our desire to reveal the character of God and introduce others to a loving Creator-God and caring Savior-Friend. And we are not alone in our desire to show a confused, dying world how to live a happy, satisfied life. But we are the ones sitting on this gold mine of information. We have material that matters. I ask again—or maybe I should say our Lutheran friend asks us again—Where are we going with this?

I chose "better plan" as part of the subtitle for this book because Ellen White uses that exact phrase, and because it captures the essence of what this book is trying to convey:

"Those who train their pupils to feel that the power lies in themselves to become men and women of honor and usefulness, will be the most permanently successful. Their work may not appear to the best advantage to careless observers, and their labor may not be valued so highly as that of the instructor who holds absolute control, but the after-life of the pupils will show the results of *the better plan* of education" (*Fundamentals of Christian Education,* p. 58; italics supplied).

It is interesting that this better plan is in relation to students becoming more internally responsible rather than externally controlled and compliant. It has to do with teachers controlling less, yet caring more. It has to do with freedom-based accountability. To be sure, a school or classroom based on freedom is more challenging to direct than a classroom based on manipulation, control, or force, but it seems that is our challenge. God has had no less challenge in directing His classroom, the universe.

As we come to the end of this book it would be good for us to reflect on the messages of the following Scripture texts. The first is such a wonderful picture of God's interest in each of us and His role in our lives: "Look! Here I stand at the door and knock. If you hear me calling and open the door, I will come in, and we will share a meal as friends" (Rev. 3:20, NLT).

We consider our homes to be private and secure, and because of that we expect people to knock on the door or ring the doorbell. Jesus uses this everyday example to portray the way that He approaches us. He is our Creator and commands the universe, yet He stands at our front door and knocks, as any stranger would do. As an all-powerful ruler He could enter on His own power whenever He wanted to, yet He waits for us to open the door and invite Him in. No force on His part.

He lets us know that He wants to be with us, but it is our choice whether we will open the door. God could make us do whatever He wanted, yet He stands on our front porch and waits. And better still, what does He wait for? Simply to share a meal together as friends. He values relationships. He yearns for our friendship with Him to be meaningful and strong. We would all agree that we certainly need a relationship with Him.

Could it be that He desires a relationship with us as well?

The devil has tried to portray God as arbitrary and selfish. He wants us to view our Creator as a God who takes but doesn't give, a God who limits our experiences and reduces our freedoms. And to a great extent he has succeeded in getting the human race, even Christians, to accept this portrayal. Think about some of the temptations you are battling with at the moment. Doesn't that view cross your mind, that God is somehow limiting you, or that a full commitment to God would hamper your life and lock you into boredom? Yet nothing could be further from the truth. Paul reminds us of the real truth: "Now, the Lord is the Spirit, and wherever the Spirit of the Lord is, he gives freedom" (2 Cor. 3:17, NLT).

These texts share the essence of what Ellen White and William Glasser are trying to say. The texts serve as beacons as we navigate through our relationships, especially as we navigate the seas of parenting and educating. The texts affirm the *power* of choice, the value of friendships and connected relationships, and the importance of freedom. Somehow in our dealing with colleagues, spouse, or children we need to emulate the example of these texts. Somehow in our managing of students we need to model what the texts are saying.

I hope that this book has an impact on your thinking. Both Ellen White and William Glasser have been prolific writers on the subject of education and effective learning strategies. Ellen White saw Christian education as a vital part of the fulfillment of the gospel commission to "go into all the world" and share the good news of hope, happiness, and salvation. Her book *Education* stands as a classic on effective teaching practice that continues to offer timely and relevant help 100 years after it was first published. Four books are exclusively devoted to the topic of education, but it becomes clear when reading any of Ellen White's material that she loved children of all ages and desired her fellow adults to join her in that love.

William Glasser has written no less than five books totally dedicated to the topic of education. His book *Schools Without Failure* (1969) argued that poor student performance was largely because of school practices and strategies; it grabbed the attention of many educators. Through many other books, journal articles, and interviews, as well as thousands of training sessions, he has patiently continued to make these points. It is because of their comprehensiveness and scope that I doubt whether a book such as the one in your hand right now can capture the important principles espoused by Ellen White and William Glasser. I worry about that. I wonder whether the right exerpts were quoted, or whether an effective explanation has been given. And of course I am concerned about accurately portraying the ideas of both authors.

In the end I will have to trust your judgment as to how you evaluate the ideas expressed within these pages. Glasser himself emphasizes that he just wants to give people information from which they can decide, based on their own experience and values. Ellen White emphasizes the need for us to be intelligently convinced of the truth. Each of us is on an individual journey. My hope is that this book will help you on your journey.

At the very least, I hope that the book will inspire you to seek educational approaches that are based on "best practice/best research." I hope you will pick up one of the "red books" and read it anew. I think you will discover an approach to learning that will surprise you. I hope you will study the ideas of William Glasser. I am confident that you will find help from his ideas that will benefit you personally as well as professionally. His book *Choice Theory* would be a good place to start if you haven't read any of his material up to this point.

Someday I think I will do a revision of this book. My understanding continues to develop as others help me refine my ideas. As I step back from this project I think some things will become even clearer to me. Before any revision of this book, though, I would like to write a book sharing the similarities between choice theory and Scripture. As with the "red books," the correlations are striking. In the meantime I will attempt to put into practice the advice that God gave to Ezekiel when He said to "let all my words sink deep into your own heart first. Listen to them carefully for yourself" (Eze. 3:10, NLT).

BIBLIOGRAPHY

Coloroso, B. *Kids Are Worth It! Giving Your Child the Gift of Inner Discipline.* Rev. ed. New York: Harper Resource, 2002.

Covey, S. *Seven Habits of Highly Effective People.* New York: Simon and Schuster, 1989.

Dewey, J. *Experience and Education.* New York: Touchtone, 1938.

Dreikurs, R. *Children: The Challenge.* New York: Hawthorne Books, 1964.

Glasser, W. *Choice Theory: A New Psychology of Personal Freedom.* New York: HarperCollins, 1998.

———. *Control Theory in the Classroom.* New York: HarperCollins, 1986 (later republished as *Choice Theory in the Classroom,* 2001).

———. *Every Student Can Succeed.* New York: HarperCollins, 2000.

———. *The Quality School.* New York: HarperCollins, 1990.

———. *The Quality School Teacher.* New York: HarperCollins, 1993.

———. *Schools Without Failure.* New York: HarperCollins, 1969.

Holt, J. *How Children Fail.* New York: Pitman Publishing, 1964.

Kohn, A. *Beyond Discipline: From Compliance to Community.* Alexandria, Va.: Association for Supervision and Curriculum Development, 1996.

Kovalik, S. *Integrated Thematic Instruction: The Model.* 3rd ed. Kent, Wash.: Susan Kovalik and Associates, 1994.

Marshall, M. *Discipline Without Stress, Punishment, or Rewards.* Los Alamitos, Calif.: Piper Press, 2001.

Roberts, M. *The Man Who Listens to Horses.* New York: Random House, 1997.

Sizer, T. *Horace's School: Redesigning the American High School.* New York: Houghton-Mifflin Company, 1992.

———. *The Students Are Watching: Schools and the Moral Contracts.* Boston: Beacon Press, 1999.

White, E. *Counsels to Parents, Teachers, and Students Regarding Christian*

Education. Mountain View, Calif.: Pacific Press Publishing Association, 1913.

————. *The Desire of Ages.* Mountain View, Calif.: Pacific Press Publishing Association, 1983.

————. *Education.* Mountain View, Calif.: Pacific Press Publishing Association, 1903.

————. *Fundamentals of Christian Education.* Mountain View, Calif.: Pacific Press Publishing Association, 1923.

————. *Our High Calling.* Washington, D.C.: Review and Herald Publishing Association, 1961.

————. *Testimonies for the Church.* Mountain View, Calif.: Pacific Press Publishing Association, 1948. Vol. 5.

————. *Thoughts From the Mount of Blessing.* Mountain View, Calif.: Pacific Press Publishing Association, 1956.

Wong, H. *The First Days of School: How to Be an Effective Teacher.* Mountain View, Calif.: Harry K. Wong Publications, 1998.